Reluctant Gu

Sitting out the war in a prisonei
wounded and captured in the D   ₁ʋ nad no
appeal for Henry Vies Suggit. Fr   ᵧ ₋ₐₗₗ ne was moved to
Germany, then on to Sudetenland ın present-day Czechoslovakia,
to a party working on the railways. Before long he and two companions had broken away on a first bid at escape. They were
eventually recaptured and returned to camp; but thoughts of freedom would not go away. Using all his ingenuity and determi-
nation, Henry Suggit went on to make several more attempts at
escape from a variety of camps until finally, in spring of 1945, he
met up with the liberating Americans.

Prison camp life, with its tedium and constant demands on the
physical and psychological resources of its inmates, is described
here with spirit and good humour; while the author turns the
episodes of escape into high adventure. A sequence of lively
sketches illustrates his account of two of the break-outs. His
German captors and guards emerge as human beings, and his
fellow prisoners-of-war are portrayed with all their strengths and
weaknesses.

Those who may have shared experiences similar to the author's
will get a lot of pleasure from this book; but anyone who enjoys
real-life adventure will like this tale of a man with 'itchy feet'.

RELUCTANT GUEST OF THE REICH

Henry Vies Suggit J.P., M.M.

JANUS PUBLISHING COMPANY
London, England

First published in Great Britain 1992 by
Janus Publishing Company

British Library Cataloguing-in-Publication Data.
A catalogue record for this book is available
from the British Library.

ISBN 1 85756 006 X

Cover design David Murphy

Phototypeset by Intype, London

Printed and bound in England by
Antony Rowe Ltd, Chippenham, Wiltshire

Contents

Illustrations between pages 51 and 52 and 89 and 90

Chapter 1

Action

Everything seemed to have gone quiet, after the terrific uproar of the previous few minutes, when all hell had been let loose. 'Anyone alive in the back?' I shouted, and a voice I recognized as the wireless operator's answered back, as I heard him clambering out of the carrier, 'I'm off.' I had the impression that he had grabbed a rifle before making his escape from the crippled carrier. I never saw him again, but believe he got home via Dunkirk.

Left to my thoughts, with movement impossible and breathing not easy, but in remarkably little pain, I fully supposed that I was finished. Here I was, in a shot-up carrier on a Belgian road, instead of being at home on this sunny Saturday afternoon! What a waste . . . what would my mother and my little Scottie, Buster, be doing? What a shock it would be when news of my demise reached home! How long this state of semi-consciousness lasted I do not know, but I became aware again of the sound of motors and guttural voices in the near vicinity. In spite of my condition and fatalistic thoughts, self-preservation caused me to call out for water, not because I was thirsty, but rather as a means of letting it be known that somebody was still alive on the carrier, and also in the hope that I did not get a quick bullet from some nervous trigger-happy German.

Faces peered over the side, and I well remember their letting out what were unmistakably German oaths, as they looked at the devastation their anti-tank gunners had caused on our puny vehicle. As they gathered round, one of them reached over the side to get the water-bottle I was wearing. It was riddled and obviously empty, so he gave me a drink out of his own; an action that gave me some confidence. A grenade box mounted above and behind my seat had become dislodged and was impeding movement of my head. Seeing my discomfort, one of them wrenched it out. Next they carefully lifted me out onto blankets spread on the ground. These were no doubt our bedding taken off the side of the carrier. Some sort of conversation took place between us, more in English than German, their command of my language being obviously better than mine of theirs. My trousers were cut away and I was stripped nearly naked. I was covered in blood and gore, no doubt more from my driver than myself! My various wounds were attended to and I was assured that an ambulance would soon pick me up.

I was so surprised at the treatment I was given, that I told one of my captors, who seemed to be in charge, to look in my tunic for a regimental badge I had managed to get before we moved into Belgium. When he produced it, I gave him it as a souvenir, an action that in retrospect struck me as funny: after all he could have helped himself to anything he wanted. I found out later that the only things they took were a pocket camera and films and my army paybook! It was not long before the promised ambulance arrived and I was loaded into it.

As far as I could tell at the time, it was a civilian ambulance that had evidently been taken over, like the hospitals, by the invader. Inside were two other casualties, Germans. One of them had been bitten by a horse, and the other had a wound in the elbow. The latter was an anti-tank gunner. I wondered if he was on the gun that had stopped us. It would have been an irony of fate if such was the case! They were both very affable and we chatted as we travelled, with me doing my best with my school-boy German. As a point of interest, although the success of the German blitz-krieg attack was principally due to the enemy's superiority in armour and speed of movement and his complete control of the air, he still used horses. Indeed many of these unfortunate animals had seen service in the British army prior to our mechanisation.

Our journey lasted about half an hour, and involved crossing one or two repaired bridges judging by the way we mounted wooden planking on our route. In due course we arrived at a hospital, and I was carried in past a crowd of curious onlookers gathered outside. My two companions must have stayed on the ambulance to be taken to another hospital, because I never saw them again. I was deposited onto what appeared to be a stone slab: it was certainly cold. After an intensive examination, I was informed that I would live! They asked me whether I had been inoculated against tetanus, and I told them I had been. I was moved to a small ward and put to bed. An injection followed and I was soon asleep.

Chapter 2

Hospital

The following day I woke up to find myself in a ward of about thirty beds. This, I was told, was the only part of the hospital with any patients, the rest of the wards having been cleared ready to receive casualties. This was a typical example of German thoroughness and ruthlessness; the bulk of the patients in this ward were in the terminal stages of their complaints and would soon be gone. I was also informed that I was the only soldier in the hospital. Unfortunately, although my wounds were far from fatal, as I had previously feared, I was completely immobile and had to lie on my back for about a fortnight, although that part of my anatomy had collected most of the shrapnel. When I did manage to get out of bed, my leg wound made movement difficult and limited my tour of exploration to a few paces outside the building I was in.

From time to time visitors to some of the patients came and had a few words with me, sometimes bringing me cigarettes, chocolate and even home-made jam, and best or worst, what I wanted most, news of the war! To convince me of the full extent of the Allied debacle, which I found incredible, they brought me newspapers. Before this, I had always maintained to the nurses and doctors that the Tommies would be coming to collect me. This I had fully expected would be so until news of Dunkirk shattered my hopes. To add to my depression, patients were dying daily. I presumed most of them must have been Catholic because priests were frequent visitors to administer the Last Rites. One male patient went crazy and the nurses had a rough time handling him, which they had to do without any male help. Incidentally this 'loony' must have taken a fancy to me, because in his chasing round the ward, he paused at my bed to give me an orange!

My optimism about being retaken by our own forces diminished daily as news of the general retreat came to me via the visitors. I could only think how lucky I had been to survive so far without being too badly damaged! I was also thankful for my choice of captors, who had behaved with such chivalry and correctness. I learnt later from other wounded prisoners that such was not always the case. As I improved, so my embarrassment increased, particularly with such treatment as bed baths. I avoided the use of the 'slipper' by saying that I 'had been', when they came round checking up. In the end, after nearly a fortnight's inactivity in that direction, I let them know! This resulted in my being given the works. They used every treatment they had, much to my further embarrassment, but without success. It was not until I was starting to hobble about, after being transferred to Hôpital Brugman, that I had any success in 'waste disposal'. It was a very painful experience.

Before leaving that first hospital, I gave two of the nurses who had looked after me a couple of my personal possessions: an engraved pocket flask and a pocket compass. The latter I knew would be of use if I attempted escape, but the odds were that I would have been deprived of it later had I tried to keep it. The rest of my belongings I did manage to hang on to.

Chapter 3

Kaputt

As my condition improved my thoughts turned to the events leading up to my present predicament. My troop, comprising three bren carriers and eleven men, had been in position as rearguard, covering a possible line of approach of the enemy. We had been a few miles from Brussels, which city we had left the previous day. As a cavalry regiment we were supposedly to probe the whereabouts of the enemy, to make contact and to report back his position and strength. That was the theory. The fact was that we and apparently the whole of the British Expeditionary Force (BEF) were left out on a limb, with, as far as we could tell, the near collapse of our allies and, even worse, no air cover. Indeed, apart from German bombers, the only plane we saw was a Lysander.

Later I learnt that this was in German hands, having been captured intact, and instead of spotting for us, was doing this job for the Germans. For our part, we seemed to be on the move all the time we were in Belgium, taking up position after position. We were convinced that the aim of this action was to give the Belgians the impression of our being in greater numbers than was the case. From time to time we appeared to be under sniper fire from an unseen enemy; in one particular instance from our own side, indeed our own squadron. The regiment had assembled in a village, and in moving out, we in the leading troop had been mistaken for the enemy by the tail end of the squadron. Fortunately there were no casualties and the mistake was soon rectified. About this time we were warned to look out for red blankets on washing lines, these being a signal by fifth columnists to where the enemy could find petrol. As the Germans advanced on the capital, the roads filled with refugees adding to the general confusion and impeding movement.

While in the outskirts of the capital we saw some of our infantry moving up to take position to try and stem the enemy's advance. As they passed a chocolate factory, girls were handing them chocolate. Some time afterwards, in the course of our flitting about, we passed what appeared to be the remnants of an infantry company who had every appearance of having had a hammering. The whole situation was chaotic, we neither knew what was happening or where we would be sent next. We were beginning to realise that something was far from good with the Allies' efforts. In spite of all that was happening around us, I managed to buy some fags with French money, in a tobacconist's. Little did I realise that in a few days' time I would be smoking some of them in a Belgian hospital. With the world collapsing around him, there was one businessman making an effort to carry on normally! Soon we were on the move again and parked up for the night in a small village. The following morning I made contact with a sergeant of the 15/19th Hussars who were on our right, but there was still no sign of the enemy.

Towards noon we were ordered to retire. Being troop sergeant, my carrier was the leading vehicle. It was not long before we reached a junction with a main road. Travelling on it was a platoon of enemy cyclists, possibly about thirty in number. Who was the most surprised I'll never know. It was an opportunity not to be missed by our Bren-gunner trooper, Arnold, a Tank Corps reservist. He took full advantage of the situation, decimating most of this easy target. In the meanwhile our driver, Corporal Griffiths, a regular 'Skin' (that is, from the Inniskilling Dragoon Guards), had spun the carrier round and back we went to the two following carriers. We were ordered to carry on in our previous direction, which we did, although had I been in charge of the troop, my TA – Territorial Army – training would have prompted me to find an alternative route. The very fact that the Germans were on bikes pointed to the possibility of heavier armed troops being in front of them. However, 'Orders is orders', and who was I, an amateur, to tell a regular Troop Sergeant Major (TSM) his job? Had I argued, it might have been misinterpreted. As it was, we had had a nasty shock on meeting the enemy at such close quarters. So back we went, retracing our original movement past the scene of the carnage we had created a few minutes previously, and turning right we tore down that road flat out ostensibly on our way to France.

On our way we passed obvious signs of the hurried departure of other units of the British Army, when we saw camouflage nets left up where some of our artillery had been positioned. The guns had been removed but quantities of ammunition had been left in stacks by the roadside. Further on were some of our sappers, who yelled out to us that they were only waiting for us to pass over the bridge they were positioned near before blowing it up.

We had only gone a few miles when, mounting a rise in the road, we saw the rear of a German convoy. We were only a few hundred yards off them, and closing rapidly. We had no option but to try and plough through them; at the worst, the two carriers behind us might manage to turn about and get away. That was what they did, as I found out after the war was over, and compared our memories of that fateful day with my pal from the volunteer Yeomanry, Corporal Sissons, who had joined the 'Skins' at the same time as me. He was the driver of the TSM's carrier. Everything was confused, Arnold was already blazing away with his Bren and my Boyes rifle added to the din. I could not help thinking, as I fired, how many will it go through? A morbid thought no doubt, but nevertheless, it kept running through my mind as I struggled with the gun's massive bolt spring. I must have been on my third magazine when disaster struck. It was as though I had received a terrific kick in my right calf as Griffiths, my driver, slumped forward, a bloody mass of erstwhile humanity. The carrier was still careering on, and I tried to get hold of the wheel with my right arm, but found I could not use it, so I tried with my left, at the same time trying to get my left foot on the accelerator. Both efforts were of no avail and our vehicle, though keeping in a straight line while on the move, soon came to a halt. We were hit twice again, and I felt a clout in my back. I have vivid memories of watching holes appearing in our armourplate.

Chapter 4

Brugmann

The time came, 4 June, when I had recovered sufficiently to be transferred to another hospital, Brugmann. My new address was a far bigger and more modern establishment. It appeared to be a series of buildings in what was tantamount to a park. Here I met a variety of races including British, French, Belgian, Algerian, Moroccan and Tunisian. From them I heard first-hand accounts of the retreat to Dunkirk, and the more I listened, the more incredible the picture became – or did it?

Was not history repeating itself for the BEF? In 1914 the Force had been thrown in at the deep end, to try and stem the onrush of the invading Germans, fighting against impossible odds as the Belgians and French retreated. Forced by sheer weight of numbers to fall back, they managed by sheer guts and efficient use of arms to delay the enemy long enough for the French to rally and between them finally to bring the Germans to a halt. The line then held remained almost the same for the next four years of the war. The derisory remark attributed to the Kaiser referring to the BEF as 'That contemptible little army', eventually became famous with the meaning reversed! Any movement of either side on that front had to be bought by thousands of lives, the tactics of attrition. Mechanisation, particularly the tank, and dive bomber, had drastically altered the balance, and no longer were heroics sufficient against an enemy superior in both these arms.

With the threat of heavy bombing, the Dutch lasted only four days, and our other two allies were soon in retreat, leaving the BEF in danger of being completely cut off and annihilated. It soon became apparent to us in Belgium that mastery of the air was not ours. From my new colleagues in hospital, I heard harrowing tales of the strafing they had undergone from the Stukas who had complete freedom of the sky. 'Where was our RAF?' was the question on everybody's lips. My unit had been subjected to some shelling from German field guns at the beginning of the retreat, and although from time to time enemy planes had flown low over us, fortunately we had never experienced their dive bombers. The distinctive intermittent throb of German bombers was unmistakable.

Our treatment in Brugmann was first class and, in fairness to our captors, I am sure was the same for all, German or allies. Most days those well enough to enjoy a glass of beer received a bottle. Smokers were not forgotten, with issues of cigarettes or cheroots. There were the odd times when these privileges were withheld as a punishment for some disregard of the rules. Gerry could be childish at times! A typical example of this was when one of our doctors was smoking in bed, in semi-darkness; as his bed was near a window, the movements of his arm and cigarette were taken to be signals. My schoolboy German got me into trouble with the Wehrmacht subaltern who had been put in overall charge of the hospital, a position that boosted his ego, given that his only qualifications were those of a medical student; but after all, he was on the winning side at the time.

He enjoyed annoying us with his victory talk and his boasting of the 'Master Race'. I, for my part, was in the habit of arguing and contradicting some of his statements. To crown it all I had picked up a catchy German tune off the wireless, some time before the war, and not realising what it was, I used to whistle it now and again. The tune was the Nazi Party song, the Horst Wessel song! His annoyance reached the limit one day, and he had me moved from the ward where my friends were to one of eight beds, only three of which were occupied, two by Belgians, the other by an Englishman who was in a very bad state with multiple wounds. Conversation was very much restricted. My compatriot was in no condition to say much, being heavily sedated and the other two spoke different languages, Flemish and French. With my smattering of German and French I did manage to get through to them, and help to break the boredom of my short stay in that ward.

A day or two later we were joined by another patient, a severe burn case, whose injuries were to the face and hands. I understood he had been at the receiving end of an incendiary bomb. He was in a terrible state; his face was like a partly melted waxwork model, and his eyes were just two blobs. He would have been in shocking pain if he had not been heavily sedated; whether this was the reason or whether his condition prevented him from speaking he never made so much as a murmur. He was not bandaged, but his treatment was some sort of salve which the nurses applied with infinite care. His hands rested on a pillow. He was fed through a corner of his mouth with one of those teapot-like containers. I woke during the first night he was with us and was shocked to see what appeared to be a bloody human head at the foot of my bed. It was his. He had staggered out of bed and collapsed in a sitting position on the floor at the bottom of my bed. I called the nurses and they soon had him back in bed. Blood was all over the place, but with admirable coolness and efficiency he was soon cleaned up.

The nurses were really marvelloous, all the more so when one considered that our part of the hospital complex was formerly for children, yet here they were, dealing with men whose wounds were in all parts of their anatomy; bullets and shrapnel are not particular! In the beginning four doctors were treating us, two women doctors and a Spanish and an Indian doctor. They were later joined by some Royal Army Medical Corps (RAMC) doctors and personnel. The two women were direct contrasts in looks. The senior one was dark and very masculine in features and hair style, while the other was fair and particularly good looking. I always likened her to one of those statues of Grecian goddesses with finely chiselled features! The Spaniard, who was the senior surgeon, was christened the 'Butcher' by our lads! The Indian was sent away by the Germans and then, after a day or two, brought back. Rumour had it that public outcry had saved him from the hands of the Gestapo. The matron, a diminutive middle-aged lady, who had trained under Nurse Cavell of First World War fame, was the real 'gaffer' of that part of the hospital. She was a real disciplinarian and brooked no interference from anybody, and that I think, included the Germans! Her nickname, the 'Sergeant Major', speaks for itself!

I had only been in that ward for a few days when she came round with my 'friend', the German commanding officer, and enquired of me how the severely wounded Britisher was getting on? I said he was responding to my attention to him, in that I had persuaded him to eat a little, and he seemed to be a bit brighter. Giving me a 'knowing look' and more or less ignoring my remarks, she explained to the German that it would be better for that patient if I left the ward. She had her own way, and the following day I was back with my companions. Before I left that section, I saw a vast improvement in the 'burn case'. He was able to eat, his eyes were open and it seemed his sight had been saved. Some time later, I and my three pals were moved to an improvised ward, with five doors leading off it, that was big enough to hold five beds. This, no doubt, was to make room for more serious cases in our previous ward.

By now, those of us who had recovered sufficiently to do light work, did a daily spell in the cookhouse, finishing off potatoes that had gone through a peeler. We sat either side of a large rectangular tiled tank, at one end of which a Belgian member of the staff kept loading a mechanical peeler, a sackful at a time. There were about twenty of us, including Belgian women. We had a hard time to keep up with the peeler. In the middle of this process, work stopped for elevenses, sandwiches, coffee and some form of conversation. For us it was a welcome break from our boredom.

I remember being asked about a bridge over the Channel. It seemed that some of the locals had been in conversation with German soldiers who were convinced that there was such a structure, and even claimed to have seen it marked on a map of that area. Our reply was that if there was one, it must be a pontoon bridge . . . some pontoon! In the light of what came out later, this fantastic story must have been inspired by the movement of pontoon-like boats the Germans were assembling in the Channel area in preparation for the invasion of England.

I sometimes was given another job in the cookhouse that required dexterity and precision: topping and tailing runner beans and feeding them into a slicing machine. The food in this hospital was good, if a bit unusual. Once a week we were given minced meat in its raw state, and likewise raw herrings, boned and in a sauce. Neither of these items were very popular and I often ate more than my share, as I found them quite palatable. In any case I intended building up my reserves, if possible, for leaner times to come, anticipating prison camp rations in the not too distant future. I was not far wrong. Those among us who chose to be fussy must have lived to regret their actions. Many never ate crusts and others almost demanded white bread, which was reserved for 'stomach patients'. The cookhouse was very modern and included steam-jacketed boilers. As it was summer, salads were part of our diet. These were prepared in these same boilers with their lids open and, of course, no heat on. Among the green ingredients went a bucket or two of sugar, which to me seemed most unusual, but my knowledge of gastronomical activities was very limited.

Shortly after our foursome was moved to our annex, we were joined by another of our countrymen. He was not wounded, but qualified for treatment by virtue of some unidentifiable stomach complaint. He was one of the RAMC personnel and had all his gear intact, even to pyjamas. Whether or not we were envious of the extra attention he appeared to be getting from the nurses, I do not really know, but we were for ever 'taking the mickey' out of him and his questionable complaint. I am almost ashamed to admit we gave him a dog's life at times. Typical of our activities was when we bounced him on his bed, using it as a trampoline. It was an angle iron-framed bed and our strenuous efforts succeeded in bending it. In trying to straighten it by reversing it and jumping on it we managed to snap it. We soon remedied this little mishap by swopping it for a spare we found in another room.

Chapter 5

French Draughts

After that episode our activities in his direction were somewhat subdued. A variety of indoor games occupied a lot of our time, and I became a bit of a spiv or expert at draughts, even with the French way of playing, which I learnt from some of the French colonial troops. One in particular, a Moroccan sergeant major, because of my bragging to him about how easy he was to beat, christened me the 'professeur'. Jigsaws were very popular, particularly the very big ones, and it was a common sight to see half a dozen or so men with arms outstretched all over the table, striving to reach their required piece! We, the walking wounded, had a lot to be thankful for when we saw some of our less fortunate compatriots with far more serious injuries than us. I came to think that they really had 'guts' in accepting their misfortune with such tremendous fortitude. In several cases it was only their courage and will-power that kept them alive, as was confirmed to me by one of the senior nurses. On the other hand, there were those with far less serious injuries that should not have proved fatal, but who nevertheless died because they gave up the struggle. One of the stoics, who really stood out among us all, was a cockney. He had lost a leg, but was always ready for a lark. We drew a face on his bandaged stump and he would announce to all and sundry that 'Arthur', the face, wanted a smoke. This tactic never failed and, though he smoked like a chimney, he always managed to get enough cigarettes to keep him going. As an instance of his gameness and the tricks we got up to, we once lifted him on to a trolley and, threatening to bath him, we pushed him at breakneck speed down the corridor to the bathroom. We never carried out the threat but were sure our victim enjoyed every minute of it. In spite of his disability and its consequent effect on his life later on, he was a 'damn good sport'.

There were others like him, who, though severely wounded remained cheerful and thought nothing of cracking a joke about their missing parts. Some of our crowd were allowed in the theatre to watch operations being performed, something I never had the stomach for. Another of the severely wounded who stands out in my memory had had something like seventeen operations by the time I left the hospital. He was propped up in bed with one leg in traction and one of his arms suspended from a frame above his bed, and still had a smile on his face. His case was yet another example of what sheer will-power could do in the field of endurance.

Our morale, as a whole, was comparatively good in spite of the news we were getting of the progress of the war and the contemplated invasion of England. Individual experiences I heard from fellow patients only confirmed my general impression of our inadequacy in all directions. Where were our leaders? Where was our air force? The Maginot Line had proved useless because our other allies had refused to link their defences up to it, and we were all paying for it now! As occupied countries they would soon realise the error of trying to be neutral. Why, when we had introduced the tank in the First World War, had we not better tanks to meet Hitler with? The more we discussed events as we knew them, the more we said, 'Thank God we have the navy'. Personally I could never understand why Hitler had not used his armour to prevent the evacuation at Dunkirk? Did he hope to get some sort of a treaty with us to join with him in his forthcoming invasion of Russia? Another question never really answered to my knowledge was who formed the rearguard at the Dunkirk perimeter.

Life in Brugmann went on, if not merrily, at least reasonably pleasantly; although obviously not as good as being in hospital back home. We were indeed fortunate in our form of captivity, not having the long march other prisoners were forced to make, laced with many examples of German brutality. While they were suffering because of the hot weather, those of us who could get about were enjoying the sun. Quite a few, like me, could not get enough, and we took our shirts off whenever we could get into the hospital grounds. This had rather painful consequences for me with plasters on my back requiring daily changing. The removal of the old ones, although done by experts, was nevertheless a hazardous experience, and I am sure the nurses doing the job had no mercy for my sunburn.

To break the monotony, I did a bit of sweeping in the grounds; though looking back, I cannot remember what I was sweeping. It could not have been leaves as it was still summer. However I had a brush and it was not only for leaning on! Anyhow it served as a disguise. One day, while I was out with my brush and getting nearer the German area of the hospital, I saw a German on a litter. Edging nearer, I could see he was reading a Belgian newspaper printed in French.

As a means of starting a conversation I said in the best German I could muster, 'I see you understand French.' My acquaintance, replying in good English, enquired how I was being treated; 'very well,' I replied, and continued, 'but I don't expect anything but rough treatment when I am sent to a prison camp, especially if I'm in one run by the Prussians.' He retorted, laughing, 'I'm a Prussian, what makes you think that?' I said I had gathered from First World War books that they were the most brutal. He assured me that was not the case, and went on to ask me my unit. This was a question I should normally have not been required to answer, but in the circumstances and after Dunkirk it was of no value to the enemy. When I told him the 'Skins', 5th Royal Inniskilling Dragoon Guards, he answered by telling me to my surprise the name of the colonel and other details. He went on to say he had broken his leg in a motor accident in Paris and that he was a major in the Intelligence Corps. We had quite an interesting conversation and then I wandered back to my quarters, pondering on the fact that he knew more about the regiment I had joined six months before than I had acquired in the same time. What a contrast he was to the young upstart subaltern who was in charge of us.

This individual had given my little group strict orders to stand to attention whenever he entered our quarters, an instruction that I almost forgot one afternoon. All the rest of the gang were laid out on their beds, while I, out of sheer boredom, was swabbing the tiled floor with a mop and bucket of water. Our mutual friend appeared in one of the doorways, and after a few seconds, while he remained glaring, I suddenly remembered our instructions. 'Oh, aye,' I shouted, 'Achtung.' That they were feigning sleep was obvious by their alacrity in jumping out of bed and assuming the required posture at the foot of their beds. It was easy to see, even to the pompous individual to whom it was directed, that we were 'taking the mickey' out of him, and with a face as red as a beetroot he ordered several repeat performances. As soon as he was gone we nearly split our sides with the laughter we had had so much difficulty in restraining during the 'punishment drill'. It was a good job he did not come back or we would probably have finished up in a concentration camp.

For me Sundays were the highlight of the week, when a military band played in the grounds for a couple of hours. Another source of music was an old gramophone and a handful of British records. What museum it and the records came out of did not matter, we had music! Included in the repertoire were 'Oh Johnny', 'Bluebells' and 'Three cheers for the red, white and blue'.

Chapter 6

Lead Swinging

There was a French patient who was pretty handy with his scissors and with his help we managed to keep our hair in trim; it was usual to reward him, if possible, and with this in mind, after he had trimmed my locks, I gave him my last piece of coinage, a French franc (it had a value of 1½d . . . possibly about 18p in present-day currency), in order to 'show willing'. Later on I was told he was a French Count. The only other money I had was an English pound note, which I gave to a nurse to try and get me a razor. She got me a Gillette and one blade which I made last for six months. Considering that for the most part shaving and washing, when we left hospital, was done without soap or hot water, it spoke well for British steel. Our outer clothing, when we were not confined to bed, was a blue woollen jacket and trousers. Footwear was in the form of heel-less slippers.

I had been taken prisoner with only my greatcoat and tunic slung over me. My trousers had been cut away, being well splattered with blood, possibly my driver's as well as my own. I had to think about making provision for the time when I would be discharged as fit for moving to a prison camp. The nurses found me some trousers, no doubt those of a patient who had died. These were saturated in blood and one of the legs had two holes in it, a small bullet entry hole and a large one where it had made its exit; otherwise they were in good condition. With patience and time, and a lot of soaking in cold water, I eventually got the blood out of them. After drying them in the sun, I set about darning the holes and finished with a reasonable addition to my wardrobe. My tunic received the same cold water treatment, but there were too many holes in the back, mostly very small ones, to do anything with.

Our 'mutual friend', the officer commanding, was a bit of a camera enthusiast (spiv was the name we gave it), and one day, when the numbers of the walking wounded on the lawn outside our accommodation were swelled sufficiently for him to get a group photograph, no doubt for propaganda purposes, he assembled us all to practice his expertise with his cameras. Our little group were together watching the performance, refusing to join the main body. However, he took a snap of us, and, what was even more surprising, he later gave us copies. A month or so previously he had taken a snap of me having a bit of shrapnel taken out of my leg, but although he showed me the photo, he never gave me a copy. I could only presume that in giving us copies of his latest efforts, he had let time mellow him. Who knows?

We used to see a fair amount of aerial activity, and one day while we were counting a flight of bombers flying in a westerly direction, he joined us. We had made the number to be sixty-four and obviously their destination had to be England. 'Oh, yes,' he said, 'England is nearly finished by our bombing and those you have just seen are going to Hull.' This was obviously for my benefit. It was too childish to pay attention to, and certainly not worthy of someone in his position. Our reply, 'How many do you think will get back?', left him speechless. He was the first thoroughly unpleasant German I had encountered and in my own little way I think I gave as good as I got.

We had similar types among our own fraternity, such as one who boasted about taking rings off dead Germans and backed his statement up by showing us some of those items. He even claimed to have hacked off fingers to get them. To have them in his possession was as stupid as his bragging, and would no doubt get him into serious trouble before he got home, if he ever did. There were others whom we could not stand near us, for a totally different reason, smell. This odour came from suppurating wounds in plaster casts on broken limbs. These casts had a window in them where dressings could be changed, and the nurses who did that job must have been real heroes – or without a sense of smell! Whenever a group of us was joined by one of these unfortunates, we would gradually disperse, and no wonder.

As time went on and quite a number of us were fit enough to be transferred to more austere surroundings, we came to be quite proficient in 'lead swinging', an art in which we were encouraged and assisted by the medical staff. However, all good things come to an end and so it was with us. The dreaded day came at the end of August, when a bus load of us were transferred to a Belgian barracks in Malines near Antwerp. Before we left we said our farewells. One of the doctors, who evidently knew about my trouble with the German officer warned me to 'keep my trap shut', in a friendly way and with a twinkle in his eye.

Most of us had only what we stood up in and could hold in our pockets, and I was no exception. Two scraps of paper I had preserved were my only souvenirs along with a couple of photos. One was out of an American magazine showing a trooper of the 5th Royal Inniskilling Dragoons, my regiment, kissing his horse goodbye; the other was a Belgian newspaper cutting showing the British Military Attaché laying a wreath at the tomb of King Albert in the name of the same regiment of which he was Colonel in Chief. For me to have found them, in the circumstances I was in, was almost incredible. I still have them, fifty years later. Part of the interest of the first photo was that, while the army was being mechanised, the Germans were among the principal buyers of our horses. Ironic, but nevertheless borne out during the war, when our cavalrymen found the familiar markings on dead horses.

Chapter 7

Malines

As the bus left the hospital grounds, we were all, I am sure, somewhat apprehensive about the future. The ride, our first chance to see the outside world, did little to cheer us up. We passed burnt-out vehicles and, as we got clear of Brussels, war-damaged buildings, and travelled over repaired bridges. German troops were everywhere.

It was not long before we arrived at our destination in Malines. The entrance to the barracks was through an arch which opened out on to what was formerly a parade ground with a First World War memorial in front of four-storied blocks protected by a barbed wire fence spanning the full width of the square.

As we dismounted and were led through a gate in the wire to what were to be our quarters, I had the feeling of depression akin to that of a prisoner facing a life sentence; and the forlorn expressions on the faces of the inmates watching our arrival did nothing to cheer me up. We were soon allocated our sleeping accommodation on the top floor of one of the blocks. Each room had a dozen beds complete with sheets and mattresses, luxuries that once we had left Malines, most of us would not encounter for nearly five years. The real shock came when we received our rations, a German army loaf of black bread to be shared by seven men, a ladle of watery soup, a few potatoes boiled in their skins, and a portion of cheese between two. This was one of those segments of wrapped cheese packed in circular packs, normally six in a box, and would do well to weigh an ounce! I was thankful that I had eaten everything put before me whilst in Brugman in anticipation of the lean times to come, unlike quite a few of my compatriots who had chosen to be 'picky' with the hospital food. After dining on half our ration, and with the remaining portion in our pockets, some of the more venturesome of us made our way down the stairs to explore the rest of the establishment we were in.

Our fellow inmates were a 'mixed bag', as in the hospital we had just left. There must have been the best part of a dozen nationalities and among the British were RAMC personnel including several officers. As our billets were on the top floor, we were able to see glimpses of the outside world and in the distance the railway on which the only traffic seemed to be military materials, guns, tanks, and vehicles in particular and all headed, as far as I could tell, back into Germany. A German field battery of six guns, horse drawn, pulled into the barrack square one evening at about eight o'clock. The horses were unhitched and trotted in pairs past the farrier sergeant who selected those that needed shoeing. The work was done there and then with the aid of a mobile forge. At the same time, hot food in the form of a thick stew was dished out to the troops lining up with their dixies while we looked on, hoping there might be some left to come our way.

I cannot remember any of our crowd touching lucky. I did not manage to get any, but I did have a chat with one of the German non-commissioned officers whose job was selling cigarette-making machinery. This, he told me, was the best in the world, but he acknowledged that we in England made the best cigarettes. I was told by one of our party who was unable to sleep that the artillery unit left at 3 a.m. We were not in our new quarters long before we made the acquaintance of the camp commanding officer, a loud-mouthed German sergeant whose ranting and raving could be heard all over the place. He was an arrogant bully of the worst type.

We took advantage of the warm sunny weather by sitting shirt-less with our backs to the wall of one of the buildings and in line with a First World War memorial. While we were pursuing this strenuous pastime one afternoon this 'whispering baritone' decided to exercise his vocal chords and clear everybody off the barrack square. While all and sundry were rushing like scalded cats to get into the compound behind the wire, we remained completely inactive. When he spotted us, as he came charging round the memorial that had up till then hidden us from his view, he nearly exploded, and let out a roar that would have frightened a lion, let alone us! I am certain that all the others out of us six were as apprehensive as I certainly was, but like me did not dare be seen to 'chicken out'. As he came round the memorial, arms flaying like a windmill, and his face red as beetroot, he confronted us, yelling at the top of his voice. As one man we rose to our feet and started to amble forward in the required direction. As we passed him he kicked out at us in turn as we got within range. In his excitement his aim was bad and the nearest he came to success was when the last of our little party was about to pass him and put his hand behind his back to protect his rear and in doing so grabbed the offending boot with the result that its owner nearly lost his balance, and in his temper drew his pistol. Fearing the worst we meandered on and through the gate, fully expecting to hear some shooting. Nothing happened, to our relief, and we made our way through the throng who were obviously enjoying the performance of this member of the 'master race'. We were told later that the principal actor of this drama, or comedy, left the scene utterly bewildered and stormed back to his office.

The sequel to this episode, which had been seen from start to finish by the RAMC doctors from their quarters overlooking the square, was an enquiry into the Commandant's brutality to wounded prisoners. The medics lodged a strong complaint. We, the 'victims', were tipped off to exaggerate our various infirmities when we paraded before the offending party the following day. For some reason or other, I never knew why, I was selected as the ringleader. He made no mistake about it when we were assembled in front of him. 'Der blonde dort' ('the fair one there'), he shouted, pointing to me. So, in the company of two of our officers, I limped across the square to the commandant's office, there to be confronted by a German officer, our 'friend' and a typical hard-faced German woman, obviously the secretary. One of our doctors spoke German and put our side of the case, which was, as far as I could interpret, that, having only recently left hospital, we were totally incapable of 'jumping to it' as demanded by the German NCO. The latter kept interrupting but was jumped on by his superior, and his look of dejection increased as the discussion went on. All the details were evidently being taken down by the woman secretary. Finally, with an exchange of salutes all round, we made our way back to our quarters.

The outcome of this little affair was the change of camp commandant. Our loud-mouthed acquaintance had lost his cushy job and
justice would seem to have been done. I do not know whose hat
the feather should have gone in, the medics, the actors (us), or
the Germans. I am content to leave that to the reader. After a
couple of weeks we were on the move again. I was better equipped
now, having bought a ruck sack with prisoner-of-war (POW) currency, cigarettes. This very useful piece of equipment had been
given to one of the other POWs by a Belgian, judging by the
writing inside it, 'Good luck, old boy', 'Antwerp'. It survived the
war but the writing was washed out, with beer, at a later date.
That's another story!

A very mixed bunch of us left Malines a day or two later in a
bus. Included among us were French and French colonial soldiers
and British from Brugman and other Belgian hospitals. Our destination was unknown to us. After an hour or two we were in
Germany and dumped for the night in a large three-storied house
just over the frontier. Our first and only meal that day was dished
out: soup and a lump of bread. Our sleeping quarters were bare
rooms with the floor serving as our beds. After a visit to the
latrines, the old-fashioned two-seater earth closet, we were locked
in for the night after being given the warning we would soon
become accustomed to: 'If anyone escapes, we shoot ten of you!'
Needless to say, this threat was never carried out – we kept too
much of an eye on each other!

The following day we were taken to the railway and entrained
in wagons, bearing the loading instructions so well known to the
'Tommies' of the First World War: '40 men or 10 horses'. By now
our numbers had increased by those already at the house when
we arrived. The wagons had two window-like openings diagonally
opposed and two bung-holes, the latter being particularly useful!
The 'windows' were heavily barbed-wired. In these cramped quarters we were only able to squat to rest our legs. Apart from an
occasional issue of soup and bread by the German Red Cross, our
only food, when the door had to be opened, and once when we
were ordered at gun point to cross the lines and relieve ourselves
near the hedge at the other side, we remained locked in for two
days. Once or twice air raid alarms caused the train to stop in a
siding, and we were given the customary warning about escaping.
By the time we got to our destination, Hemer, near Dortmund,

we were all proficient in the use of the bung-holes. I should point out that among the forty in the wagon were twelve men with only one lung. The only prisoners to travel in carriages were those who had lost a leg.

Chapter 8

Hemer

We were marched, or should I say we ambled, to the prison camp at Hemer, Stalag VI A, where we were detailed off in groups of twenty for the purpose of drawing rations. Food in the form of bread and a sort of salad was issued. Then fortified by this 'rabbit-meat' we were distributed to our sleeping quarters for the night – marquees! They were not exactly luxurious, but at least we could stretch out on the ground unlike the previous night spent in the confines of a railway wagon. These tents were erected in a barbed-wire enclosure just outside the main camp.

The following day we underwent registration as prisoners of war and were given our official numbers. It was hardly a comforting thought to know that, until this procedure had been gone through, we could have been 'bumped off' and no one at home would have been any wiser. Only after this paperwork had been completed would we have any protection through the Red Cross under the 'Articles of War' recognised by both belligerents. Even so we were to be POWs for nearly a year before we heard any mention of the Geneva Convention on the treatment of prisoners of war.

It was not part of our military training to learn how to demand correct treatment under this treaty, if and when one became a guest of the Reich. Being taken prisoner was one risk we never gave a thought to, although we knew that being killed or wounded was on the cards. To complete the formalities of initiation we were all issued with a German army 'dog tag' with our number on it.

When all this was over, we joined the happy throng in the main camp and were shown our sleeping quarters. The buildings were unfinished army barracks four storeys high arranged round a parade ground with a single-storey cookhouse situated off centre, so as to cater for all the barracks and still allow parades to be held in the main area. Our billet was at the top of one of these blocks.

The sight that met us as we entered stunned us. The floor was strewn with straw, and sleeping areas on it were marked out with bricks: the latter served two purposes, holding the straw in and marking out the occupant's claim to territory. A scene of feverish activity took place wherever a 'bed' was in use. At first it struck us as being funny, but we knew very well that it would not be long before we would be doing likewise. Lice are no respecters of dignity. Diarrhoea was rampant as could only be expected with the filth all of us were subjected to, and the almost complete lack of washing facilities. A tap and trough outside the building was all we had. The diet did not help, being principally watery soup and bread. The cookhouse had twenty serving hatches and we were formed up in columns, ten abreast, to collect our daily issue, with German guards releasing us in twenties to tear off to the nearest empty issuing hatch. During the time I was there our numbers had swelled so much that the cookhouse was unable to cater for all; so a mobile kitchen was brought into the square to help. It was a large trailer about thirty feet long on which two steam-jacketed boilers were mounted. Even with this additional cooking facility the Germans were stretched to the limit to cater for our swollen numbers which were in the region of 30,000. It was not unusual to see a big hose-pipe topping up the boilers while their contents were being ladled out. Hunger was so rampant that prisoners raking among the peelings in the cookhouse dustbins was a common sight.

In their utter dejection many were searching in their Bibles for a prediction for the future, and some startling theories were produced. They found mention of a beast and a bear and likened these to Hitler and Stalin. Even in September 1940 there was talk among us of the possibility of war between Germany and Russia.

In the same camp were Poles who had already been prisoners for a year and were far better organised than us and the other allied POWs. They were housed in one of the blocks opposite ours, and, as far as I remember, never drew rations with us. I became friendly with one of them, a sergeant in their Tank Corps, who came from Lodz. He started me on the rudiments of Polish, and gave me a hand-written dictionary based on American English. They had certainly got themselves clean and tidy billets, and were able to write home and receive parcels as well as mail from Poland. To supplement their rations, their relatives sent them whatever food they could spare, and consequently they were in far better shape than the rest of us in that camp. They gave me to understand that there was some sort of scheme under which some of their number had been repatriated, but I gathered that if they took advantage of it, they were liable to be conscripted again and on the wrong side.

My contact with them was soon cut short, as all the British in the camp were being assembled in one of the blocks in readiness for a move. Just as the company I was in was being moved to this new assembly point, I was in the throes of dysentery and, while being helped by a friend, Bob Cowper of the Yeomanry, I collapsed and finished up in the camp sick bay. I learnt afterwards that it was due to Bob's insistence that I needed medical help that I was taken to this camp hospital. All I remember about this episode was his helping me to find the lavatories in the new block, and our both struggling to step over men lying in the straw while he kept striking matches to allow us to see. Filthy and rough as that camp hospital was, I am sure Bob's action saved my life.

With the departure of the British contingent I found myself the only Britisher in 30,000, but at the time it was of no consequence. French personnel appeared to be running the sick bay with the assistance of one German doctor. For the best part of a week my time was spent sitting on a bed pan on top of my bed, during which time I hardly slept at all. For food I was given a concoction of semolina that reminded me of wallpaper paste. From time to time it was varied by a tasteless form of macaroni and a chunk of white bread. I hardly touched the bread putting it under my pillow where I am sure a mouse used to nibble it.

During the long sleepless nights I could hear what I took to be the RAF giving its attention to Dortmund in the distance. At midnight I was given an injection by one of the orderlies, who had been roused by the German guard. In my semi-conscious state I remember being given a daily glass of red wine and I was of the impression that the German doctor sent out for a bottle every day and the French were giving me a glass and supping the rest themselves. That they were not the trained personnel they purported to be soon became obvious to me. No doubt some of them were genuine, but the others had doubtless faked their pay book entries. . . . To them it was a cushy billet, a haven of comparative comfort, that afforded opportunities of increased rations at the expense of the patients. I was in there a fortnight in a filthy condition as befitted a sufferer with dysentery, without having a wash or clean up. When not using the bed pan or slipper, I passed time folding bits of newspaper (supplied for obvious purposes), and catching lice off myself, dropping them in the fold of the paper and running my thumb down the fold to see the pattern made by the blood – mine – that had come out of them.

My clean-up came when a British sergeant, a newcomer to the camp, came into the hospital. Seeing my predicament he acted in true 'good Samaritan' fashion. He even took some of my clothing away to clean. If I ever knew his name I have forgotten it, but I am forever in his debt.

To supplement my meagre diet, I was fed glucose by injections in my thighs with a monster of a syringe which produced massive lumps until they dispersed into the blood stream.

I gradually began to come round and take some interest in the goings-on in the sick bay. One of the French orderlies had been a professional artist before the war and kept his hand in whenever he saw a suitable subject. His humorous sketches included one of a black French soldier carrying a slipper at arm's length with his other hand holding his nose! He did brilliant portraits, and some of his technique rubbed off on me when later I ventured into this field and found I had some ability. I never tried his method of ink studies, however: these he did with a sharpened piece of wood dipped in ink. Another Frenchman in the ward acted several times as a sitter for the artist, who I think, like me, was fascinated with the artistic tattoo this man carried about on his torso. How anybody could go through life with such an obscene tattoo covering one side of his body I could never understand.

Towards the end of the month I was pronounced fit enough to join the other British who had assembled during my stay in the sick bay. My weight had gone down to seven stone from a norm of about ten and a half, and I had the strength of a mouse when I left the luxurious surroundings I had been in, to wind my way back into the main camp and into the building allocated to my compatriots. Somehow I managed to climb the stairs to the top floor where they were, and was almost in a state of collapse on arrival.

I had been in 'dock' the whole of October and now we were into November and the weather had changed with the month to rain and fog. We felt the cold intensely; obviously our poor diet was the main reason, being hardly enough in quantity and quality to keep us alive. Coupled with our primitive accommodation it was dragging us down to a state almost akin to the notorious death camps. In spite of the conditions, most of us struggled to preserve some of the spirit that the Germans were trying to sap out of us. Having seen the way the French orderlies in the sick bay were living, I managed to get past the guard to that compound on several occasions and prevail on the racketeers to give me some of their ill-gotten gains to supplement my diet.

Chapter 9

Lamsdorf

After coming out of the camp hospital and back into the main camp, I found the conditions even more grim. The weather became cold and wet with the onset of a German winter, and in our efforts to keep warm we wore all the clothing we could muster, looking more like zombies than soldiers.

Towards the end of the month we finally left that camp, shuffling to the station and entraining once again forty to a cattle wagon. This time we were issued with rations: a loaf, half a tin of bully beef and a quarter of a Red Cross parcel. My share was the packet of tea and a tin of milk powder. I ate the milk, which set like concrete on my spoon and teeth. The tea had to wait till we got to our destination three days later. During that time we were never let out of the wagons. Water was given to us during the various times the train came to a standstill, no doubt to let more urgent traffic through. In the three days we were on the train the German Red Cross managed to get soup to us on two occasions. Our previous experience with the bung-holes was again put to the test. In hospital we had been treated like human beings; but now, in spite of us all recovering from wounds, we were treated like cattle when travelling on the railways.

I had managed to get a place near a 'window' and whenever I could muster the strength to stand and overcome the cramp that set in with squatting, I could look out at the terrain we were passing through. For the most part the scenery was drab and uninteresting; pine forest or open country. Now and then we were halted to let faster trains through, mostly troop trains.

Some of the lads had pocket chess sets and they were put to

good use. While we were not despondent, neither were we full of *joie de vivre*, and spent a lot of the time deep in thought.

Eventually we arrived at Lamsdorf and were lined up and set off for the camp. This comprised single-storey concrete buildings set in groups in a series of wired-off compounds, all within a main perimeter which was a double fence about eight feet high, with a gap between of about five or six feet filled with tangled barbed wire. Look-out posts every fifty yards or so equipped with machine guns and search lights were manned day and night. The camp administration had offices inside the main gates, and entry to the camp was through more gates about a hundred yards from the main access.

Once inside the camp we were split up into companies and allocated to the building destined to be our home for the unknown future. Our beds were two-tier wooden bunks with a straw-filled palliasse supported by seven bed boards that rested on two runners inside the wooden bed frame. Two blankets completed the job. Each of these buildings was heated by a massive tiled stove with a very small fire aperture, the bulk of the structure being really a winding chimney designed to extract all the heat possible before the smoke left it. This is a system commonly used on the continent, especially in the colder parts, of which Silesia was certainly one. Our supply of very inferior coal was, like our rations, cut to the bare minimum. When it lasted long enough to warm the stove, this became a focal point for all lucky enough to get near it.

A common practice with our issue of boiled jacket potatoes was to mash them in whatever we had to serve as a dixie and put the container in one of the flues in the stove to warm up while we gossiped. The danger was, that if we let our eyes and minds wander off our cooking, it in turn would walk. Food was a constant topic of conversation and many elaborate menus were devised by the epicureans as they reminisced about the good old days in England. My thought was that this activity only made our position worse by serving to increase our desire for food and draw attention to our inability to do anything about that part of our lot. As for myself, although I was in a slightly better condition than when I left the sickbay, I realised I had to do something drastic if I was going to survive, let alone escape, which thought was forever in my mind.

We had been at Lamsdorf a week and were getting into the routine when the Germans came round, drawing up lists of names for outside working parties. Hearing that miners got heavy rations, I put myself down as a miner. I had never seen a coal mine, let alone been down one, but I was prepared for anything if it might help me get fit. A few days later I found myself on a mining party of fifty, and being a sergeant, the senior non-commissioned officer on that party, I was put in charge. We were lined up to march to the station, and one of our party who had a smattering of German was appointed *Dolmetscher* or interpreter. On the way to the station he must have been jostled out of position near me by a Liverpud-lian who professed to having a better command of German. Our guards were a *Gefreiter* (lance corporal) and two privates.

Chapter 10

Morgenroth

At the commandant's office we were halted and an officer came out to inspect us and our documents. I was in a bit of a quandary. I had to salute. In getting into this working party I had not mentioned my right arm, which had not recovered from a nerve injury that made opening my right hand difficult. In hospital I had managed to write and shave with my left hand, and the Indian doctor, Assurappy, had told me that only concentration would bring it back to anything like normal proficiency. He pointed out that in his country the fakirs learnt to wag their ears by continued concentration. I could grip with the offending hand, but opening it was difficult. On the spur of the moment I saluted with my left hand, taking a chance that it would not be noticed. It paid off, no one noticed, and I breathed again.

The trip to our destination was uneventful and took about three hours. There we were shepherded into a big detached house with barred windows which was adjacent to the mine in which we were to work. The front door led into a hall, on the left of which was the kitchen; next to it further down the hallway was the guards' room. Immediately opposite was a corridor with two bedrooms on each side, and at the end was a small bedroom.

We were sorting ourselves out among the four main bedrooms, and I was busy with the bed I had just selected, when one of the lads came to tell me that the self-appointed interpreter had installed himself in the small bedroom, along with his chum. Life in a prison camp was a bit like the jungle in the early days, and little regard was given to stripes. Any form of authority was established either by will-power or physical means. Whereas the

Germans respected my stripes, others among ourselves did not give a tinker's cuss for them. I had to act, and quick, if I was going to have any say among the present party. I stormed into the little room as the two culprits were beginning to sort out their gear. Without saying much, I claimed my bed, the top one, (there were two, one on top of the other). The *Dolmetscher*'s chum had no alternative but to go and find himself another billet. Hardly a word had been spoken but I considered I had won the first round.

After we had settled in we were given a meal, stew with some body in it and moreover on plates! This was a considerable improvement already. Beds with sheets, plates to eat off, stoves in every room and obviously ample coal to burn: this really was luxury! My interpreter was sullen and subdued after my exercising of authority without recourse to argument.

Next we were issued with overalls and divided into two shifts. Working times were 6 a.m. to 2 p.m. and 2 p.m. to 10 p.m. The shifts worked alternately, week and week about. Sometimes we worked above ground, generally when they were short of wagons, but for the most part we were underground (*untertag*). At night the whole of the above-ground workings were fully illuminated, indeed our first sight of the village was the fully lit up Christmas tree complete with coloured lights. We were out of range of our bombers, and Russia was not yet in the war. We were, in fact, very near the point where German forces first entered Poland after an incident staged to give them an excuse for invading. Some of the frontier pillboxes were in the precincts of the mine. The locals used a dialect which seemed to be a mixture of Polish and German.

The morning after our arrival my shift reported for work and descended the 320 metres to the bottom in the cage after being given our acetylene lamps, which burnt a naked flame. The part of the mine we were working in had no gas. Once at the bottom, we had to walk a fair distance to where a group of miners were gathered, waiting for instructions from the overseer. When the miners had been allocated the area in which they were to work, we were detailed off to the little groups of miners. We then walked some distance further into the mine, following our new work-mates.

Once at the coal face we kept out of the way while the miner and his assistant prepared to blast the coal down with explosives. The miner set about drilling the coal face with an electric drill, first with a metre drill and then with a two-metre bit. This done, he placed the explosives in the holes, complete with a detonator wired to them. Behind these he rammed clay rolled into sausage-like shapes by his assistant. The wires trailing out of the borings were then joined to a long length of wire, at the end of which was the generator. Next we followed the professionals to the full extent of the wire down the corridor. We had to stand close to the wall and facing away from anticipated blast. A warning shout was given in case anybody had been missed, 'Brennt'. With a twist of the wrist on a knob on top of the generator the explosive was set off. First came the bang, then the rumble of falling coal and then the clouds of dust, which we had to let settle before anything else could be done. The miner was the first to go and inspect the newly created space, paying particular attention to the roof, tapping it with a miniature pick to make certain it was solid and there was no danger of any fall of loose coal or rock.

The road to the face had narrow gauge lines to take the tubs as near the face as possible, and we were allowed to make a start on loading. While this was going on a couple of old-timers were laying another length of line nearer to the working. In the meanwhile the miner and his helper were extending the roof shoring right up to the face. The whole procedure went like a well-oiled machine, with no one getting in anybody else's way. Halfway through the shift we stopped for 'elevenses', something we had not anticipated nor been prepared for. However, our new workmates shared whatever they had with us, in true comradely fashion.

Before loading the tubs, the miner made sure one of his numerical tallies was slotted through the hole in the end of each tub. Thus, at the end of each shift, the tally of coal sent up was credited to the correct miner. As we were novices and not very fit, the miner and his helper lent a hand with the shovelling, so that by the end of the shift the coal face was clear for the next shift. As far as I can remember, once we were fit, thanks to the improved diet and conditions, we had no difficulty in averaging something like twenty tubs per shift, the tubs holding something like a ton. The size of a normal coal face was around fifteen feet wide by seven feet high. I never remember working where it was necessary to stoop.

At the end of the shift we showered and left our overalls suspended from chains and hoisted them up to the roof of the bath-house ready for wearing on our next shift. At the start of a shift we reversed the procedure, leaving our clean clothes on the hooks. The Germans religiously counted us entering this building and again when we came out. Our lamps we took back to the billets to replenish the carbide and water. To light them we had cigarette lighters used without fuel as only the spark was required to light a lamp. We were able to use naked flame lamps because we were mining only low-quality coal. It all seemed to be going to Italy, possibly in exchange for their wine and tomato products. There was no mistaking the Italian wagons with their gable end construction.

Other jobs we were put on included working on the surface particularly when there was a shortage of wagons. We also had to tip tubs of mine waste, slag, on to one of those massive heaps seen wherever there is a pit. On occasion we might be loading tubs with bricks destined for some job down the mine. We could not help indulging in a bit of sabotage in these last two jobs. Sometimes we tipped the tub overboard on to the slag heap and buried it with slag; and where loading bricks was concerned we became expert in the art of breaking as many as possible as we loaded the tubs.

We had only been on the job a couple of days or so, when the *Gefreiter* came into the little room I shared with my interpreter and started to give him some instructions. Feigning sleep, I listened to the one-sided conversation, and when the lance corporal had gone, I enquired of my interpreter what it was all about. All I could get out of my linguistic expert was something about our party having to use the mine 'loo'. I let him sweat a bit, not being able to make head or tail of it. Telling him he had not got a clue, I asked him what the box of little bottles was for? Again he had not a clue. I sacked him there and then and found one of our party who had a better knowledge of German, more or less on a par with my own. The episode with the bottles and the mine lavatory was simply that the Germans, always afraid of epidemics, required samples of faeces from all the party. The toilets at the billet were a two-seater earth closet situated outside the building. Those at the mine were water closets. Their design, with a kind of tray in them, considerably facilitated the procuring of a sample with the aid of the spoon on the end of the bottle cork. It was a

fiddling task which we all had to undertake. We never heard any
more about it after we had completed it.

My new interpreter was Ben Miller, a native of Lerwick in the
Shetland Islands, and a corporal in the Gordon Highlanders. We
struck up a partnership and worked together down the mine as
well as in the billet, both having the intention of escaping when
the time was right. With this in view we prevailed on a mine
electrician to get us a hacksaw blade to attack the window bars
with. This little effort of getting the saw took us the most part of
three months, so frightened were most of the locals of being found
out helping us.

Between us Ben and I almost took charge of the party. We
organised a canteen for them where they could spend their allowance pocket money, and when anybody went back to the camp at
Lamsdorf they were paid up to date before leaving. Most of our
stock for the canteen was bought from a little corner shop near
the mine which was authorised to take POW money, *Lagergeld*.
By making a small profit on the transactions we were able to bribe
the guards and in return we had them bend the rules to the
advantage of us all. One of the first consignments of food from
the Red Cross that came our way was a crate of condensed milk.
Following the rules rigidly, the guard commander made us open
every tin and deposit the contents into a bucket. We only did this
once; a bottle or two of beer worked wonders after that episode.
Another time some of our party were in dire need of footwear,
having only wooden clogs to work in. When we pointed this out
to the guard commander, he assured us that the mine owners had
plenty of boots. With his help we prevailed on them to distribute
the footwear needed, and create the post of cobbler for one of the
party who qualified.

Teeth were another problem. Quite a few of us visited the local
dentist. I myself had a tooth filled, requiring three visits. Anyone
with a gold ring to spare could have a gold filling. Not only did
we get boots, but we were issued with German army underclothes:
not a patch on ours but very acceptable nevertheless. We also had
our laundry done for us, though no doubt we were paying for it
out of the deductions for our food and lodging.

By the time Christmas came, a fortnight after our arrival at
Morgenroth, we were well settled in and beginning to feel like
human beings again. Christmas day was a holiday, and our treat

for dinner was an extra sausage and some sort of improvised dumplings in the stew. The previous night I had been given a change of job in the mine. With a Polish lad, who was a bit 'wanting', we were given the job of loading the three bins out of the mine lavatory into one of the tubs, before sending them up to the surface. They were full of slop, reflecting the prevailing diet in Germany during the war. Somehow they had to be lifted into a tub. Seeing a pile of bricks nearby, I managed to make my helpmate understand my intention, a difficult job considering he was not all there. We set about building a stepped-up ramp with the bricks alongside the tub. Then we very carefully worked one of the bins up the 'stairs' and lowered it into the tub; no easy job because the tubs had rounded bottoms! Repeating the procedure we managed to get the three bins loaded without spillage.

Christmas over, the new year, with the temperature dropping every day, found us working more and more on the surface, with the snow piling up every day and creating difficulties with the supply of wagons. Up to this time quite a few of the party were still wearing wooden clogs. It was only when our friendly guard commander told us about the availability of boots, and backed me and my second-in-charge up when we confronted the mine directors, that we got them to issue boots to all requiring them.

Another outside job we had was helping to fight a fire that had started in a mountain of coal stacked near the pit before the war. Spontaneous combustion had set it alight, and several of us had the job of shovelling it, in an effort to get at the seat of the fire. The temperature was minus 20°C and the water dripping from the big hoses used to try to stem the fire formed huge icicles from the nozzles. Meanwhile the shovellers were standing on hot ground. I had a spell at this work but never knew the ultimate result.

On another occasion a gang of us had assembled on the top for work and the snow was coming down thick and fast, making visibility difficult. All we wanted to do was to take shelter, so we all piled into an open hut, to the consternation of the poor guard. Ranting and raving, he succeeded in getting his gang out of the shelter only to lose them again in the blinding snow. They had filed out of one hut into another nearby. He repeated the performance and so did his gang until in the end he gave up trying. During this very cold spell I saw a heavy locomotive with its front bogey derailed. Railway engineers succeeded in putting it back with massive hand-operated jacks.

Women were working in the open air, albeit under a high roof, in what they called a *Separatur*. This was a conveyer belt that allowed them to inspect the coal for slag and bits of wire, that they picked off before it was loaded into the wagons. Needless to say, they were muffled up to the eyes, as they needed to be at this time of the year. On their feet, which in turn were well wrapped, they only had the heel-less type of slipper commonly worn on the continent.

The miners we worked with were very friendly and often brought us cakes baked by their wives. These for the most part had very little taste, simply because of the lack of proper ingredients. They tried to make up for this by the fancy ornamentation they put on them.

Right from our first time of working in the mine, the true Poles among them would do their best to keep us abreast with the news. One thing they were never in doubt about was the forthcoming German attack on Russia. Whenever we were working 'on top' we could see rail and road convoys heading into Poland, incorporating men, guns, tanks, lorries, portable buildings, and closed wagons no doubt loaded with ammunition. It all pointed to a big build-up somewhere in Poland. These movements went on right up to the actual attack in June. How could it have come as a surprise?

Neither myself as senior NCO nor Ben Miller as interpreter was excused work by virtue of occupying these positions. We did, however, get some privileges, including access to a drink or two in the local general store where we did most of the shopping, and sometimes a drink with the guards over a game of cards. In doing our shopping we turned a blind eye to some of the purchases, as long as the guard commander helped us improve the lot of the party by disregarding some of the restrictive rules, such as the opening of all tins in Red Cross parcels.

The arrival of a wagon-load of these, a couple of months or so after we had settled in, heralded a pretty regular flow of such welcome additions to our diet. I had the privilege of breaking the seal on this first consignment and I still have it. Another improvement we brought about was in receiving our pay at the end of the month it was earned in, instead of a month in arrears. This meant that anyone leaving the party and returning to camp never left more than a month's pay in credit: a credit he would never get. We were even able to keep books and thus allow a certain amount of 'tick'. Whatever it cost to oil the works, everyone was better off in the long run.

The erstwhile interpreter tried to stir up trouble for Ben and me by calling a meeting of the entire party one Sunday evening. As I entered the room with my number two, our 'mutual friend' was busy rabble-rousing, making me feel like Mark Antony giving his speech over the murdered Caesar. This was the only quotation from Shakespeare I could remember from my schooldays, and then not the whole of it. How well I put the case to that assembly can be judged by the result. I, or should I say we, because Ben Miller was included in the criticism, came out of that room with a resounding vote of confidence, and the former interpreter and his mate were completely dejected. They never again caused trouble.

For recreation we organised a theatre, crude, but a good diversion. The play, *Night must fall*, I wrote from the story told to me by one of the lads who had seen it. The old lass in it had a wig we had made from the string off Red Cross parcels, and it created a laugh or two. Another play was *Rope*, again written from a story told by someone who had seen the play. For those who felt the need, we held impromptu Sunday services, based on the Army Prayer Book most of us still had. As the year progressed, and with finer weather, we organised football matches on an area of ash-filled ground near our billet, and with a real football.

Letters began to arrive for some of the lucky ones in the party, followed by some book parcels. From the type of reading material that came, it seemed that some of the lads' relatives were subscribing to a book scheme at home and the organisers were unloading unsaleable issues in these parcels. The quality was not in dispute, but the subjects were only of interest to intellectuals in the remotest of subjects. It really was a racket at the expense of the POWs and their relatives.

We had neither wireless nor newspapers, but nevertheless we kept abreast of the news with the help of the Poles we worked with. When imparting the news down the mine, we would go down an old working, put our lamps out, listen for anyone coming, and only when we were sure that it was safe to whisper would our informer disclose his bit of news. Such was life in a police state.

Chapter 11

Mining

While we were all settling down to the routine of the mine work and our leisure activities, Ben and I discussed our real objective, escape. Having got hold of a hacksaw blade we set about putting it to use on the bars of our window. Our difficulty was finding the opportunity to work without interruption, our door being more or less open to all. The guard commander often popped in with some instruction or other for the party. Any of the lads with a problem was at liberty to seek our help; and of course sawing steel bars was not done without some noise! Our progress was slow and, to cover up what cutting we had managed, had to be foolproof. Boot polish solved this little problem. Over a period of time we had been able, with the help of the Polish shop proprietor, to change our POW money for German currency. For food on our projected excursion, we had in the beginning saved bread, but with the advent of Red Cross parcels that was no longer a difficulty.

Our friendship with the guard CO made us feel guilty to some extent, but duty was duty and our freedom was part of it. I wondered how the *Gefreiter* would fare when he discovered our absence. We often played cards with him in the guardroom over a drink of beer, and during these sessions I could not help thinking 'what if he could read my mind?'

When we went shopping at the little store, we generally managed a drink of beer, sometimes from the proprietor, and occasionally from the drayman delivering it and even the guard himself. Other visitors to the shop included the local police, and it was an incredible experience to be drinking in such company and looking at trainloads of military personnel and equipment piling into Poland for the coming offensive against Russia.

One character we met working in that mine we christened Chunky, not knowing his real name. He was a middle-aged Pole who had been 'a bit of a lad' in his younger days. He showed us with some pride a newspaper cutting with a photo and an account of one of his earlier escapades in which it had taken eight police-men to hold him. He was an avowed 'red' and hated the Germans. He was sure that sooner or later the Gestapo would come for him, at their favourite time in the early hours of the morning when he would be in bed. In anticipation of this he said he always kept the bedroom door locked with a wardrobe propped against it. Near at hand, he had ready his chosen weapon, an axe. We knew he wasn't bluffing! Another character I well remember was a little Polish lad who whistled the tune of our National Anthem, which he had learnt from listening to the British radio. We nicknamed him 'God save the King'.

A tune I learnt, complete with words, was always played on the wireless before a special announcement (*Sondermeldung*). The song was 'Gegen England' and we often sang it with the word Deutschland substituted for England, as we were going to or from work. Another favourite was 'Rule Britannia', which in the circumstances did not really ring true. One piece of equipment that we lacked in the first month or two was the miner's protective helmet. Eventually the mine directors were persuaded to issue them to us. We had a monthly clothing parade, when any deficiency could be rectified and our 'clothing cards' marked up with the cost to be taken out of our pay. Our commanding officer sat at a table dealing with these records while I called out the names as the men came forward to collect replacements. It was not long before these roles were reversed with me sitting at the table. I was given photos of this activity by our guard CO and likened them to advertisements showing 'before' and 'after'; in this case before and after we, the prisoners, took over. I was later deprived of these photos when we had a new set of guards.

After two or three months letters started to arrive from home for the most fortunate members of our party. I was not among them, as I had to wait almost a year before I heard from my mother. The day I got a letter I was working on the surface with Ben as a partner. We were dodging the column, ducking and weaving in and out of the various buildings, when we were told by the lads that the *Gefreiter* was looking for us. When eventually he caught up with us, instead of a complaint about our evasive action, he approached us with his face beaming, and presented me with that first letter. From it I learnt that in the early days I had been posted killed, then later missing believed killed, and it was not until mother got the letter I had sent from Brugmann that she knew otherwise. Then she had some difficulty in convincing the authorities that I was alive, and in the end she had to send them my letter to prove it to them.

As the reader can judge, conditions on this party were good, and although the work down below was hard, we had a lot to be thankful for. With this in mind, I put to the men the idea that we make a collection for the invalids in the camp at Lamsdorf. They gave it their full support, and the money was sent by registered post. I still have the receipt to this day.

With the approach of summer I had ideas of organising a party to go swimming. I did not know what facilities were available locally, nor the official attitude to such a daring scheme, but I was quite optimistic that I could pull it off, providing Ben and I were still there. I kept this idea to myself, not wishing to raise hopes too soon. The proposal would have been intended not as a jumping-off effort for escape, but as a genuine attempt to improve life further for the party. I was quite prepared to have suggested individual paroles to be given by the would-be participants in return for the privilege.

Events outside our little world livened up, and this idea never got off the ground. I had been in town with the *Gefreiter* shopping for a variety of things not stocked in the local shop. With apologies the guard CO said I must walk in the gutter, as was the rule. This I did to spare him a ticking off by any jumped-up Nazi Party official we might have encountered in the town. In the course of our shopping I saw a notice to the effect that Hitler's deputy, Rudolph Hess, was due to speak at a rally in the area that weekend. This was within a day or two of his flying to Scotland.

In one of the shops we entered, the assistant tried to be clever in saying *Gefangener* (prisoner), and making the 'hands-up' gesture of one who surrenders. My escort replied that such was not the case; I had been wounded, and to demonstrate his point, he asked me to turn round. I obliged and he showed the would-be 'smart

Alec' my tunic, in the back of which I had counted forty shrapnel holes. Leaving my verbal assailant crestfallen.

Chapter 12

Guards Change

Within a week or so, we had a change of guards and a new commandant. He was an *Obergefreiter*, a sort of two-stripe lance-corporal, and one step higher in rank than our first. He was slightly younger than his predecessor but not old enough to have seen service in the First World War, nor had he seen action in the present war. He was a typical *Heimatsoldat* (home service soldier), a stickler for the rule book, which I was certain he studied continuously. Against my better judgement I dropped him a hint, more or less saying, 'If you leave things running as they are, it'll be better for us all.' He nearly exploded, and, blue in the face, fumbled for his automatic. By the time he had got the holster-flap undone and drawn it, he contented himself by waving it under my nose. Fortunately for me he did not fire it but ranted and raved that he was in charge and he would brook no interference. From that moment on, things tightened up and I only had to look at him for him to start fumbling for his gun. I had to get away from that job before he blew his top. There was not room for us both on that party so something had to be done about it!

To make an escape attempt in the circumstances would have given him an ideal opportunity to rid himself of the nuisance I was becoming. My safest way was to 'go krank' (feign sick), which I did. When my shift went to work, I put on my act, stopping in bed, playing on my wounds. As soon as the workers had gone, I got up and passed the time playing cards with the lads who had come in. I was obviously flouting him, but his rule book said my fitness or otherwise was a matter for the medical people. As I was complaining about old wounds in my back, I was sent in the company of a guard to a hospital in Kattowitz where I was X-rayed for remnants of shrapnel in my back.

Once back in the billet I set about sewing the German currency that we had acquired at the local shop into my clothing and Ben's. I had to wait till he came off shift to work on his tunic. He was asleep before I had finished the job and I never had a chance to explain where it was secreted because I was wakened early the next morning by the guard and given a minute or two to gather my gear before setting off for Lamsdorf. The move was so hurried that the guard had had no time to shave, and so he left me with the German military police on the station while he smartened himself up.

On arrival at Stalag VIII B, after he had reported the safe delivery of one *Gefangener* at the camp office, we parted company, and I found my old bunk above that of Bob Hoe of the Yeomanry. Bob was an old friend of mine who lived in the same part of Hull as myself. He was a keep fit enthusiast, but not too interested in escape.

We were now in the month of July, approaching the best time of year for 'open air travel', especially if one anticipated living off the land. I became friendly with a Warrant Officer 3 from the Tank Corps and a corporal from the Durham Light Infantry. I was never really sure of his rank, as it was quite a common practice for prisoners of war to promote themselves by a stripe or two, ostensibly to fool the Germans and later on to avoid being sent out on working parties. It took about a year for us to learn one or two points about the Geneva Convention, such as that non-commissioned officers were not obliged to work as prisoners of war.

These two new-found friends had the same intentions as myself, to get away at the earliest opportunity. They had made some preparations to go as a trio, but the third member had scalded his hand and had to drop out. Why it was so important to go as a trio I didn't bother to enquire, but I jumped at the opportunity when asked if I would take his place.

Chapter 13

E211

We dropped our ranks and joined a working party destined to work on the railway at a place called Triebitz in Sudetenland. On 15 August 1941 we joined fifteen other inmates on party number E211, and after a train journey of two or three hours arrived at our destination. The building that was to be our home while on that job was a two-storey farm-type building with our quarters in the upper half. There were two windows with vertical bars and barbed wire stretched horizontally across them. Whether or not our two guards were quartered in the bottom half of the building we never found out.

The following day we were set to work on the railway, tightening bolts in the fish-plates and packing ballast in between the sleepers. We had ideas of train jumping, so often seen in films, particularly as there was a gradient and junction running in the general direction of our proposed route, south. A railway workers' hut nearby looked promising for a bit of gear.

Our day's work over, we were given a meal and shortly afterwards locked in our room and left to amuse ourselves. Before we were locked in for the night we had to put our trousers and boots outside the door. This presented us with our first setback. However, we had three pairs of civilian trousers between us and two pairs of spare boots, so we were only short of one set of footwear. Up till then, nobody on the party knew our intentions, but learning that the sergeant in charge of the party had the necessary spare pair of boots, we confided in him and he volunteered to put them out as our third pair and recover them in the morning before the Germans discovered their loss.

We decided to go the following day, our second there. Our billet was at one side of a road, and at the other side was a lake. I could not resist the chance of a swim and after work got permission to have a dip.

The evening dragged on and eventually all went to bed, ourselves included. We had bunks near the window selected for our exit. These were two tier. I occupied the bottom one on the left and my fellow plotters had the one on the right. After a long wait until the volume of snoring had reached a crescendo sufficiently loud enough for us to assume all our bed mates were fast asleep, we tackled the wire on the window and, by continued bending to and fro, succeeded at long last in breaking it. Now came the critical moment with the bars. Not wishing to draw attention to ourselves, we had only measured them with our eyes. Were they far enough apart to get through? They were, and after stealthily dressing and checking our rucksacks for passage through the bars, we knotted blankets from our beds together. With one end fastened to my bunk, we lowered the other end to the ground outside. I think the order of descent was Corporal Pugh first with his boots round his neck, then the three rucksacks, followed by myself and TSM Perry in the rear. In our journey to the ground we had to pass a downstairs window with a wooden shutter over it, not knowing whether the guards were quartered in the room behind it.

We gathered our gear and put some distance between us and the building before donning our footwear. Hardly daring to whisper, we walked in the dust-filled gutter to deaden the sound of our boots. I am sure all of us experienced the exhilarating feeling of being free, as we made our way along the track where we had been working. Coming across the hut we had earmarked, we broke in by pulling boards off the back, and helped ourselves to coats. Walking along the line we came to the junction and gradient where we anticipated jumping a train.

After about half an hour we heard one approaching. It was headed in the right direction. So far so good; but to our chagrin it did not slow down sufficiently for us to jump it. So much for the films! We decided against waiting and set off walking down the line. The first part of our plan had misfired and in the circumstances it was imperative that we put as much distance as possible between us and our former depot.

'Shanks's pony' was our only alternative. It was a lovely moonlit night and we were experiencing freedom! We had made the right decision, as it turned out, in not waiting for another train, as nothing passed us on that line as we walked through the night. With the approach of daylight, we edged away from the track and, finding a small wood, hid in it. Our intention, now that rail travel had not proved easy, was to walk at night and sleep in the warmth of sunlight during the day. In theory it seemed a good plan, but in practice it was not quite the same. With neither map nor compass, we had to keep close to the railway where possible. As long as it ran in something like a southerly direction we could not be far wrong. In any case we had not given up the idea of getting a lift on a train.

Our first and most dangerous hurdle was over, getting away from our guards on the party, who in their anger and humiliation would no doubt have manhandled us. Indeed, if we had been caught in the act they could have shot us with impunity. Unlike our military personnel, Germans were not encouraged to use kid gloves in their handling of prisoners. Fortunately not all of them took their orders to the letter, as I found out before the war ended. Cases of shootings of prisoners of war were rife in the camps. Incidents where the victims were left hanging on the wire fence or out on the ground where they had fallen were not uncommon. Leaving bodies in such a manner was considered to be the ultimate deterrent.

TIME: 8 A.M., MONDAY, 25TH
AUGUST 1941

THE ARBEITSKOMMANDO
(WORKING PARTY), EIGHTEEN
STRONG, LEAVES THE LAGER,
STALAG VIII B LAMSDORF, AND
TAKES THE TRAIN AT
ANNAHOF, EN ROUTE FOR
TRIEBITZ, SUDETENLAND.
AFTER SEVERAL CHANGES
AND AN ENJOYABLE JOURNEY
OF ABOUT SEVEN HOURS
THROUGH SOME VERY
PRETTY COUNTRY WE ARRIVE
AT TRIEBITZ AND HAVE SOME
SOUP AT THE STATION.

THEN WE MARCH TO OUR BILLETS.

HERE WE WASH AND SWIM IN THE LAKE, KNOCK APPLES OFF THE TREES AND GENERALLY SETTLE DOWN.

THE NEXT TWO DAYS WE WORK, AND

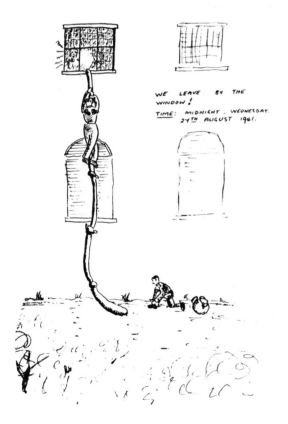

WE LEAVE BY THE WINDOW!

TIME: MIDNIGHT. WEDNESDAY. 27TH AUGUST 1941.

ON THE THIRD NIGHT, AFTER PACKING OUR BAGS, TYING BLANKETS TOGETHER, AND CUTTING THE WIRE WE LEAVE BY THE WINDOW!

TIME: MIDNIGHT, WEDNESDAY, 27TH AUGUST 1941.

AFTER A HALF HOUR WALK
WE ARRIVE AT RAILWAY
WORKERS' HUT AND
COMPLETE OUR WARDROBE!

FINDING THE TRAINS
IMPOSSIBLE TO JUMP WE
DECIDE TO WALK, AND SET
OUT ON THE LINE TO BRÜNN.

THE FOLLOWING DAY WE HIDE IN A SMALL WOOD, AND REST, WHILE CIVILIANS WORK IN THE FIELDS A FEW YARDS AWAY! LEAVING THE RAILWAY WE USE THE ROADS AND WITH THE AID OF THE 'PLOUGH' AND 'NORTH STAR' WE HEAD SOUTH SOUTH EAST. WATER IS EASILY FOUND AND ONLY TOUCHED IF RUNNING.

AFTER 2 OR 3 DAYS
TRAVELLING WE FIND
DIFFICULTY IN HIDING OUT,
AND WHEN ONE OF US HAS
TROUBLE WITH A BEE-HIVE WE
MOVE ON AND CONTINUE
WALKING – BY DAY.

WE SOON GET USED TO THE
CIVILIANS (CHILDREN AND
DOGS ARE THE WORST!).
WE REST AT NIGHT NOW AND
SOME OF THE SLOPES WE
SLEPT ON WERE 30°. ONE
MEMBER HAS A HAIRCUT.

VIEWING AN APPARENTLY EMPTY HOUSE WITH THE IDEA OF SPENDING A NIGHT THERE, ENDS IN A TACTICAL WITHDRAWAL TO THE WOODS.

LATER WE SEE WHAT APPEARS TO BE A HOUSE IN PROGRESS OF BEING BUILT, AND WE MAKE FOR IT. ENTERING IT, WE SEEK A 'NIGHT'S KIP' IN A BEDROOM.

WE AWAKE THE FOLLOWING
MORNING TO THE SOUND OF
HAMMERING DOWNSTAIRS.
HASTILY DRESSING, WE
DESCEND AND ARE CAUGHT
BY A WORKMAN WHEN TRYING
TO LEAVE.

WE EXPLAIN AND THE WORKMEN,
WHO ARE CZECHS, GIVE US THE
REMAINS OF THEIR BREAKFAST.
HAVING EATEN WE GO ON OUR
WAY AND ARE SHOWN HOW TO
FOLLOW THE CORRECT FOREST
PATHS BY MEANS OF THE
COLOURS MARKED ON THE
TREES.

WE SET OUT AND SEE, AFTER A
FEW HOURS WALK, THE FIRST
VILLAGE OF THE FIVE WHICH WE
ARE TOLD LEAD TO BRÜNN.

STILL FOLLOWING THE COLOURS WE ARRIVE
AT THE FIRST VILLAGE (SMALL TOWN),
WHERE WE REST AWHILE IN A SMALL PARK.

SEEING A SMALL SHOP NEARBY
I VENTURE OUT.

I BUY 2 KILO TOMATOES,
3 JELLIES, 6 MATCHES AND AM
SERVED BY AN OLD LADY AND
HER NEARLY BLIND SON. MY
STORY AROUSES THE PITY OF
A CUSTOMER TO THE EXTENT
OF A SLICE OFF HER LOAF OF
BREAD.
RETURNING, WE EAT AND
THEN CROSS THE RIVER BY
SOME SOLDIERS AND ON.

SLEEPING IN THE WOODS BY BOTH DAY AND NIGHT ACCORDING TO CIRCUMSTANCES. WE MEET THE RAILWAY AGAIN AND INVESTIGATE WAGON TALLIES BY THE LIGHT OF LOW SIGNALS. NOT FINDING A SUITABLE TRAIN WE CONTINUE ON OUR WAY TO BRÜNN KEEPING NEAR THE RAILWAY.

WHILE PROWLING ROUND A SMALL STATION-YARD WE HAVE TO SEEK HURRIED SHELTER BEHIND SOME STACKED TIMBER, BECAUSE OF CIVILIANS LEAVING AND BOARDING A TRAIN.

ON PAST ANOTHER VILLAGE WHICH WE MISTAKE FOR BRÜNN BECAUSE OF ITS MODERN BUILDINGS. THE ROAD WAS A SPLENDID NEW MOTOR ROAD AND ON THE RIGHT WERE A RIVER AND THE RAILWAY. CROSSING THE FIRST BRIDGE WE CLIMB THE HEIGHTS AND STOP TO WATCH A TRAIN GO BY, 50 FEET BELOW!

WE SPEND THE NIGHT ON THE TOP IN AMONG SOME YOUNG XMAS TREES. THE FOLLOWING DAY WE CONTINUE AND ARE NOW WELL IN THE MOUNTAINS WITH THE RIVER AND RAILWAY BELOW US IN THE RAVINE. BREAKFAST, SARDINES AND BISCUITS IS EATEN 100 – 200 YARDS FROM TUNNEL GUARDS AND TWO WOMEN PASS BEARING GREAT LOADS OF BRUSHWOOD.

EVENING FINDS US BY A STREAM IN THE MOUNTAIN FORESTS.
HERE WE CLEAN OURSELVES AND PREPARE COFFEE AND PORRIDGE.

ANOTHER NIGHT OR TWO IN THE FORESTS AND WE NEAR OUR DESTINATION NO. 1, BRÜNN, WHICH WE CAN SEE FROM ON HIGH.

THE FOLLOWING DAY WE SEE A REFRESHMENT 'KIOSK' IN THE HILLS AND I BUY BEER AND 'MACCAROONS'. THE PROPRIETOR ASKS QUESTIONS AND WHILE I ANSWER THEM MY COMPANIONS MAKE OFF (NOT SPEAKING GERMAN).

I CATCH UP TO THEM AND WE ENTER A SMALL TOWN. AFTER DRINKING IN A GASTHAUS WE LEAVE AND HAVE TO WAIT A FEW MINUTES WHILE A UNIFORMED OFFICIAL TURNS HIS CAR ROUND. WE MOVE ON TO THE OUTSKIRTS AND LEAVING MY PACK WITH MY COMPANIONS IN A WOOD I ENTER THE TOWN TO INVESTIGATE ITS NAME, ETC.

RETURNING TO OUR RENDEZ-VOUS AN HOUR OR SO LATER. WE SPEND A NIGHT IN THE WOODS, AND MOVE ON, ACQUIRING FRUIT (PLUMS AND APPLES) EN ROUTE.WE ARE NEAR BRÜNN NOW AND FINDING A GRADIENT, TRY TO JUMP A TRAIN.

TRAIN SERVICE IS NEARLY ALL
WEEK-END PASSENGER SO WE
DECIDE TO WAIT AND WATCH.
FOLLOWING DAY I DRESS IN
BEST JACKET AND ENTER
VILLAGE. QUEUE UP TO BUY
CIGARETTES AND BUY RATION
– TWO!
WALK AROUND CHURCH,
CIRCLE BACK AND ENTER
GASTHOUSE. HERE AM ABOUT
TO TALK TO TWO OBVIOUS
CZECHS WHEN THIRD ENTERS.
I CONVERSE AND ONLY
EXTRICATE MYSELF BY
LOOKING AT THE CLOCK AND
HURRIEDLY DEPARTING.

PAUSING TO LOOK IN SHOE SHOP
WINDOW I MAKE CERTAIN AM NOT BEING
FOLLOWED, AND SO BACK TO WAITING
FRIENDS, SEEING PROCESSION ON THE
ROAD. AM NOT BELIEVED AT FIRST WHEN
I PRODUCE ONLY TWO CIGARETTES. ARE
UNABLE TO JUMP TRAIN SO WE MOVE ON
SLIGHTLY WEST OF BRÜNN,

AND MY PALS HIDE THEIR PACKS PRO-TEM IN BUSHES NEAR NEW HOUSE.
WE GO ON TOUR OF INVESTIGATION

AND I FALL OUT FOR A SLEEP.

MY PALS RETURN AND WE WALK BACK TO THE 'CACHE'.

HAVING RETRIEVED THEIR
PACKS MY PALS AND I
CONTINUE OUR WAY,
INTENDING TO TRY THE
RAILWAY EAST OF BRÜNN.
WHILST EATING CARROTS WE
ARE INTERRUPTED BY AN OLD
MAN WHO RAVED AT US IN
CZECH AND REFUSED
PAYMENT FOR HIS CARROTS.
WHEN HE STARTED SHOUTING,
WE 'MOVED OFF' AND PASSED
THROUGH THE PLACE WHERE
WE HAD FIRST TRIED THE
GASTHOUSE.

STILL FOLLOWING THE
RAILWAY WE FIND AND
SAMPLE MORE CARROTS,
ETC., PACKED FOR
TRANSPORT.
WE AGAIN ENCOUNTER
TROUBLE WHEN GETTING
APPLES AND 'RETIRE TO
UNPREPARED POSITIONS!!' BY
ABOUT 2 O'CLOCK A.M.

WE ARE HALFWAY THROUGH
BRÜNN WHEN A DARK SHAPE
COMPLETE WITH LAMP HALTS
US AND SPEAKS IN CZECH.
SAYING WE ARE GERMAN
FACTORY WORKERS GOING
ON SHIFT, WITH FOOD AND
TOWELS, ETC, IN OUR PACKS,
WE ARE ALLOWED TO
PROCEED AFTER A PERUSAL
OF THE RUCKSACS!!

FOLLOWING DAY A GASTHOUSE IS AGAIN SAMPLED AND A 20 MARK NOTE CHANGED. WHILST REFUSING TO SELL BREAD WITHOUT CARDS THE BAKER'S WOMAN GIVES ME A PIECE WHICH WE EAT WITH FRESH BRAMBLES!!

TRAVELLING THROUGH
FORESTS WE SIGHT A HOUSE
WHICH TURNS OUT TO BE A
VILLAGE, THROUGH WHICH WE
QUICKLY PASS, SPURRED ON
BY COMING RAIN AND NIGHT.
WE SHELTER IN AN ORCHARD

AND AWAKE NICE AND WET AT ABOUT 3 A.M. PASS AN HOUR OR SO EATING PLUMS AND WITH POCKETS FULL OF FRUIT MOVE ON.

BY 6 A.M. WE FIND A HAVEN AND RETURN TO SLEEP – WHICH WE DO ON AND OFF FOR 24 HOURS WHILE THE RAIN CONTINUES AND FARM WORKERS COME AND GO, WITH DOG.
IN THE FORESTS AND FIELDS OF BOHEMIA AND MORAVIA ARE MANY SHRINES.

WE PASS WHAT APPEARS TO
BE A MONASTERY AND SPEND
A GOOD NIGHT IN A HAYSTACK,
NEAR A CHURCH. NEXT DAY
WE SEE A FACTORY
COMPLETE WITH RAILWAY AND
WE FOLLOW THE LINE UNTIL
TOWARDS EVENING

WE REACH THE MAIN-LINE. NARROWLY MISSING
TROUBLE WITH A CROSSING-GUARD WE RETURN
AND AWAIT EVENING IN THE WOOD. AT DARK WE
BOARD AN ITALIAN COAL TRAIN. AFTER SEVERAL
HOURS TRAVEL AND ESCAPING DETECTION WE ARE
FINALLY 'FOUND' BY RAILWAY EMPLOYEES

TIME: FRIDAY A.M.
13TH SEPTEMBER

LUNDENBURG.

AND SUFFERING FROM CRAMP STILL, WE ARE
TAKEN TO A TRAFFIC OFFICE. ON THE ARRIVAL
OF THE POLICE WE ARE 'FRISKED' FOR ARMS –
HANDCUFFED WITH CHAINS – MYSELF IN THE
MIDDLE, AND MARCHED THROUGH THE SILENT
TOWN WITH A GUARD OF FIVE OR SIX. AFTER
QUESTIONING WE ARE THROWN IN SEPARATE
CELLS, WHICH ARE ALREADY FULL OF CIVILIANS.

AT EXERCISE I CHANGE MY CZECH
MONEY FOR GERMAN. AFTER SIX RATHER
HECTIC DAYS WE ARE TAKEN AWAY BY A
GUARD – THIS TIME MILITARY, AND
EVENTUALLY, TOWARDS EVENING,
ARRIVE AT STALAG XVII B, A FRENCH
CAMP NEAR KREMS. WE EXCHANGE
'CIVYS' FOR FRENCH KIT AND SPEND 13
DAYS HERE BEING KEPT IN THE 'BUNKER',
AWAY FROM THE FRENCH, ETC.
WHENEVER WE GO ANYWHERE AN
INTERPRETER COMES WITH US. HERE WE
ARE LISTENING TO A SERBIAN BAND.

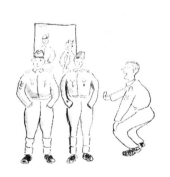

AT LAST A GUARD FROM OUR CAMP ARRIVES. WITHIN AN HOUR OR SO,
WE ARE ON THE WAY. THE FOLLOWING EVENING AFTER MUCH
TRAVELLING, CHANGING TRAINS AT VIENNA, NIESSE, ETC, WE ARRIVE
BACK AT OUR STARTING PLACE – AND 10 DAYS!

TIME: 8 P.M., THURSDAY,
2ND OCTOBER 1941.

LAMSDORF.

Chapter 14

Freedom

On the brighter side, here we were, after a cold night, quickly warming up in the sun, and with a few miles under our belts on the way to freedom. Our temporary hide-out on the edge of a wood, with a ripened crop of corn on the other side, was being laid open to the public gaze, for although we thought we were pretty safe, we had not contemplated early morning workers in the fields in the shape of women working round the edges with sickles, no doubt making a clearance for a reaper. Although they must have seen us, they took no notice of us, seeming to be oblivious to our presence. Possibly it was not an uncommon sight to see strangers lurking in the fields. Maybe they took us for conscripts dodging the draft. Whatever the reason, the fact that people had seen us without rousing an outcry gave us courage – or cheek – to continue our progress in daylight instead of waiting for nightfall.

We resumed walking, and our optimism improved as we went on. We struck across country using the sun as our compass. Inevitably we encountered villages on our way, and where possible we circumnavigated them, but others we had to pass through 'brass necking' it. Our biggest menaces were children and dogs, whose curiosity was a source of embarrassment and inward alarm. They were more inclined than adults to take more interest in us.

An amusing incident happened when we were taking a rest in a small copse of trees. Sitting among the leaves and other vegetation that carpeted the ground, we noticed an odd bee or two flying about as if searching for somewhere to land. More and more appeared and seemed intent on getting to the very place where we were sitting. They buzzed around, and in the end we had to move, so persistent were they. It appeared they had some sort of hive in the mound we were seated on. This amusing incident served to relieve some of the tension that inevitably affected us all as novice escapees in that vast police state covering nearly all Europe.

Although August came to an end and September began while we were on the loose, the nights were very cold, particularly when the sky was clear. On quite a few occasions when the sky was cloudy, the rain made conditions even worse. Sleeping in the open air in only the clothes we wore was difficult, and even more so in the hilly parts of Czechoslovakia. For the most part we had to sleep with our feet against a tree to prevent us from sliding down the slopes. To try to keep warm we huddled together; the one in the middle had the best of it.

My two companions were as different as chalk and cheese. TSM. Perry was very cautious, whereas Corporal Pugh was impetuous and inclined to take risks. Between the two I had the unenviable job of trying to keep them on the 'middle path'. Moreover as the only member of the trio to know some German, I was pushed into some tricky situations. I well remember our coming across a house some distance outside one of the villages. It seemed to be empty. We never found out if it was because, as we ventured in single file to explore it, Perry leading, myself in the middle and Pugh bringing up the rear and spurring us on, a very big Alsation sprang out at us the full length of its chain. It was near enough for our leader to feel its hot breath, so he said. Needless to say, we all took to our heels. It was a wonder the chain did not break, or that whatever held it at the other end did not snap. It was all of five minutes before we stopped running! We had a good laugh at our antics, but I could not help thinking how near to disaster we had been.

After a few days on the loose, we came across a house in a clearing in a forest, in the final stages of construction. It proved to be empty and this time without the protection of a dog. We entered and made ourselves as comfortable as we could in one of the upstairs rooms. Our intention was to rise early and make ourselves scarce before any of the workers came. The comparative comfort of lying on wooden boards, which, though harder than the ground, were dry, and of having a roof over our heads, and so not waking up, as we had at times, wet through, must have caused us to oversleep. Although the time was nearer six than seven, we woke to the sound of hammering downstairs. Making as little noise as possible we crept downstairs, only to be met at the bottom by three or four workmen. By gestures and a bit of German coupled with the words England and English, we made ourselves sufficiently understood for them to offer us what remained of their breakfast. What was even more important, they gave us a route which would take us through villages and towns with the least risk of running into Germans.

The way was comparatively simple: coloured markings on walls or trees wherever the paths diverged. The one we were to follow was two horizontal blue bars with a white one in between. As far as we remembered, these colours were similar to those of the Royal Corps of Signals. That name, the 'Sigs', stuck with us all the time we were following that trail. With a bit of luck this method would take us to Brno, passing through five villages on the way. 'Brum', as we called Brno, seemed a likely place to jump a train. So, after thanking our hosts, we set off again and felt encouraged by our first real contact with the locals.

All went well and after an hour or two we came to the first village. The road ran alongside a small river and led us past a small public garden with a memorial to the First World War in the form of a German helmet on a pillar of rock. Taking advantage of a seat in this small haven of rest, we pondered on our next move. The tinkle of a shop door bell, as customers went in or out, drew our attention to a little grocery on the opposite side of the road. Our bright spark Pugh, who was good at 'making bullets for others to fire', suggested a visit to it might produce something in the form of food. As I was the only one who knew any German, I was delegated to try my luck. Not wishing to be drummed out for cowardice, I smartened myself up, and, putting on the most respectable jacket among us, I set off into the unknown. We knew that food was rationed, but we might nonetheless be able to buy something or other to eat. Besides we had German money burning holes in our pockets.

Crossing the almost deserted road, I entered apprehensively. The shop appeared to be run by an elderly lady and her middle-aged son who was almost blind, judging by the manner in which he felt his way around. The language barrier was no real problem as they spoke German. Not having any ration card limited me to only unrationed commodities, tomatoes, jellies and matches. Another customer in the shop, hearing me enquiring if I could purchase some bread, borrowed a knife and cut a hefty piece off the loaf she was carrying and gave it to me. Whether or not she guessed I was on the run, I shall never know, but she must have known that I was not German by my accent. Thanking her and the 'old lass' behind the counter, I recrossed the road to my fellow conspirators.

After we had banqueted on the bread and tomatoes, leaving the jellies for later, we were fortified for the next stage of our journey. Meanwhile a platoon of German infantry had rolled up on the other side of the river. They had stacked their rifles and left one of their number on guard while they rested. Some of them amused themselves firing a Very pistol into the river to stun the fish. It struck me as a novel way to catch fish. Shortly after our meal, we set off to follow our sign again, but to our dismay it led us across the bridge and past the sentry with the stacked rifles. To hesitate would have been disastrous, so we ambled past him, trying to look as though we were going about our business, whatever it might have been. No notice appeared to be taken of us, although we were expecting at any second a shout of 'Halt'. We did not dare to speak to each other until we were out of sight of the sentinel.

After that followed an uneventful day's walk along country roads lined with fruit trees, mostly plum, with here and there an apple tree. It was a sight that surprised us. We could not imagine such trees remaining unmolested in England, but here the fruit must have been left intact until it was ready to be harvested. Props supported the heavily laden branches, that were sagging under the weight of the fruit they bore.

As evening came we resorted to the woods again, to hide up for the night. This part of Bohemia and Moravia was heavily forested. As usual, the following morning found us up early and on the move again as soon as we could thaw out and shake the cramp out of our bones. As the day progressed we warmed up with the sun, and now and then rested, trying to make up for sleep lost during the night because of the cold. To supplement our meagre rations we took advantage of the fruit and maize which grew in abundance in the area we were then walking through. I do not think any of us had eaten Indian corn before, and when we tasted it in its natural state and just ready for harvesting, we possibly overdid it. We ate until its very sweetness sickened us. My only earlier encounter with this corn had been as a child when I had used it as ammunition for my peashooter.

Our route led us to a village, and once again we were in touch with the railway, a contact we had lost for some time while we were still following the 'Royal Signals' trail, as we called it. By now it was dark and really our time for looking for somewhere to sleep. Following the railway, we came to some sidings with wagons assembled on several tracks. On the side of these wagons, held by a strong spring, were what could only be described as destination cards. The easiest way for us to read them was to remove them and use the light from shaded lamps fitted in between the lines as some form of signals, or aids to shunting. None of the names we found on them rang a bell, and after trying to read quite a few of them, we gave up. We could only guess what sort of chaos would result from our efforts with the cards the following day, as we were not fussy which one went where when we replaced them.

In continuing our search for a suitable place to spend the night, we found that what we had taken for a village was really a small town with a military barracks, which we had to pass. To make it look as though we were not trying to hide our presence in the dark, one or other of us smoked a fag. We went through this place without seeing anyone, perhaps because it was nearly midnight. Eventually we got clear of all forms of habitation and after some difficulty found cover in a small copse near the road and spent a huddled night together.

The following day we were up early – the cold saw to that – and continued our hike to Brno. Finding water on our travels was not a problem; any clear running water sufficed, whether it was a river, stream or even a field drain. Our main difficulty came when passing through towns. We had started our journey with a fair amount of provisions we had saved from Red Cross parcels, including chocolate, biscuits, sardines, oats, coffee and some bread. Nevertheless, we had to husband our supplies carefully, not knowing how long we would be. Hence we lived off the land as much as possible. We were all smokers in moderation, and I think at that time I was the least addicted to the weed. As with our other supplies, we went very carefully with them, only having a smoke now and again as a special treat. Our journeying that morning led us back to the railway and eventually to a station. There we noticed sawn and trimmed tree trunks waiting to be loaded along with other stacks of sawn timber, as we mooched around the station yard in our usual search for a suitable piece of rolling stock in which to hitch a lift.

The arrival of early morning passengers caused us to seek cover among the stacked timber until they had boarded their train and departed. Had we had a bit more knowledge on the subject of travelling as passengers, this might have been a different story, although in the light of later events, I doubt if it would have ended much differently. As it was in the 'citadel' of wartime Europe travellers needed a multitude of documents.

Leaving this place our hike took us through different country and on well-made roads with a narrow river on our right, along-side which was the railway. This in turn was bounded by rocky crags, surmounted by young fir trees. Now and then we passed buildings that looked like factories and were pretty modern in design. After we had gone several miles we came to a bridge over the river, which we took advantage of and crossed the railway to climb the crags. On reaching the top we found ourselves in what appeared to be a Christmas tree nursery. Here we decided to spend the night, although the ground was more stones than soil, and not the most comfortable to lie on. It provided good cover, however, and we had the sound of trains passing frequently as a lullaby to sleep. The following morning we saw that the trains had a large letter V painted on the front of the locomotive and on their sides and tender. This slogan prevailed wherever we went: 'V for Victory against Bolshevism'. I often wondered who was first with 'V for Victory', Goebbels or Churchill. Another well-used slogan on the railways was 'Wheels must roll for Victory'.

The next day found us moving through hilly or even mountain-ous terrain with a fair sprinkling of woods and forests. The railway could be seen down below, now on our left, and disappearing into a tunnel through the high ground our path seemed to be leading to. We called a halt near where the path turned into the forest and had lunch, if that is what a tin of sardines and a small packet of biscuits between three hungry hikers could be called. While we were eating two women passed us, both carrying large bundles of dead brushwood on their backs, ignoring us completely. Down below we could see the guard on the tunnel entrance pacing to and fro. He was easily within pelting distance, had we been saboteurs. If such had been our intention we had had even better targets in the train drivers the previous night!

We kept moving all day without seeing anybody and by early evening we were in what might have been an ideal picnic area in peace time. It was a truly scenic setting, with here and there very large boulders and a mountain stream running through it. The trees of the forest were thinned out enough for the evening sunlight to stream through them, creating flashes of light on the moving water. It was a scene worthy of any artist's portrayal. Recently felled trees were waiting no doubt for winter removal. Here we thought it safe enough to light a fire to have a brew up of coffee and a meal of porridge. We did not dare, however, to keep the fire going as darkness descended, much as we would have liked to. With porridge and coffee in our bellies, it was one of the best nights we had in the open.

The next day we plodded on again through similar country and while on the top of a height, by standing on a boulder we could see in the distance a large town or city, which we were sure must be Brno. It was hard to believe there was a war under way as we feasted our eyes on the beauty of it all in that late August – or was it early September. Brno seemed to be nestling among the hills.

On climbing one of these hills we came to a sort of refreshment kiosk in what must have been a picnic area. It looked as though it was open for business, and again my intrepid companions pushed me into trying out my German in another shopping venture. I succeeded in buying three bottles of beer and three macaroons, of which there was a tray full, but I dared not ask for more.

While I was paying the stall keeper, an elderly man, and after my two companions had ventured out of the bushes they had been hiding in, to collect the beer, I was questioned as to why I was not in the army: it was almost an interrogation. My answer was to the effect that I was unfit. I followed that up with a description of what I thought of the *Wehrmacht* in the best and ripest German expletives I knew. With that I made off in search of my heroic vagabond friends who had made themselves scarce. I soon found them guzzling their beer and munching their macaroons in the bushes. We did not linger about that place, not knowing what the old fellow might do. I was sure he would think we were deserters.

Our equipment was improved by each of us having an empty beer bottle, making us a bit less dependent on finding water. Our spirits were given a bit of a boost, either by our evasive action with the stallholder or perhaps the beer. Whatever it was, later in the day we ventured into a pub, no doubt to quench the appetite one bottle had given us. We each had an enjoyable sit down and a glass of beer, followed by a fag.

As we were leaving refreshed, we saw a uniformed man struggling to turn his car in the narrow road outside and assisted him with hand signals. His uniform was that of a party official, brown with a swastika armband. We certainly were getting braver; or was it again the beer? When we were scouting in the more populated areas, my German was invariably the excuse for my being delegated for reconnaissance. It did have its little rewards in the form of an odd pint or two on my own. On the other hand it had its hazards too, one of which was particularly alarming. I had entered a pub in a small town and sat with my pint some distance away from a small group of workers who were in conversation at a table. From the sound they must have been Czechs and not Sudeten Germans.

I knew the occupied countries each had an underground movement. The real problem was how to make contact with it. We knew the Germans put 'stool pigeons' in prisoner of war camps to keep themselves informed on anything unusual going on. Had we not been obliged to disguise our real purpose on the working party we had just left not only from the Germans, but also from our own people? If I had dropped these apparent Czechs a hint, how could I convince them I was genuinely a prisoner of war on the run? At the back of my mind all the time was a nagging doubt about involving other nationals. The risk of punishment we ran was nothing like the risk to them. For the most part our *Strafe* (punishment) was a few days or weeks in a camp 'bunker'; for them it could easily be a bullet or torture, and even repercussions on their families. On the other hand, my real purpose in being in this pub was to make contact. All these thoughts ran through my head in the few moments I hesitated.

In the meanwhile the little group had been joined by a newcomer more or less as I made my opening move. 'Any of you speak German?' I asked and had an immediate reply from the one who had just come in; 'Yes, what of it?' I was nearly caught off balance by his sharp authoritative riposte, but managed to say I wondered where I might get some fags. 'You know they are rationed,' was the answer snapped back at me in the same forceful tone as before. My reply, in the best German I could muster, was to the effect that there might be other ways and means. He was obviously taking too much interest in me, so, having nearly finished my pint, I swilled the remainder down, and with an almost theatrical gesture looked at the clock over the bar. Trying to make out that I had 'overstayed my leave', I made for the door, calling out as I left, 'Wiedersehen', which I followed immediately with 'vielleicht', (perhaps). Maybe I was a bit cheeky, but the words came out instinctively. In any case my parting words should have been 'Heil Hitler'. As I walked down the street I fully thought I would be followed, but dare not look back, as that would have been too obvious. Passing a Bata shoe shop with a large plate glass window, I stopped ostensibly to look at the exhibited wares, but really I was looking at the reflection angled in the window, to see if I was being followed. To my great relief I was not.

I was glad to get back to my partners, who were not very interested in my account of my little adventure, asking only 'Where's the beer?' Our trek continued and on the way we tried the railway again. It had the usual gradient, and we watched passenger trains go by with no signs of slowing down and waited long enough for a goods train with several open wagons, but, as before, it proved far too fast to jump.

In a little village, on another of my scouting adventures, I saw a queue outside a street kiosk. Joining the line of would-be purchasers, I found they were buying fags. Dodging about a bit so I was last to be served, I made my purchase, the princely number of two. Returning to the rest of the gang, I pointed out that as I had had some beer earlier, to even the job up a bit they could have the fags between them. They were a really ungrateful couple after my intrepid efforts on their behalf. I was sure they did not believe I had only been able to buy two. After they had finished their smoke, we set off again into the unknown. It was not really as bad as that; even if we had smoked our last, we were all experiencing the intoxicating feeling of freedom, something that has to be tasted to be fully appreciated. A civil prisoner let loose after serving his time comes out into the world with possible problems of surviving financially, but is not among an enemy populace speaking another language. Every minute on the loose one was pitting one's wits against the odds. Not only had we to try and avoid recapture, but we had to find sustenance as and when our meagre supplies ran out.

Chapter 15

Brno

In this fashion we made our way to Brno, not that this city was the end of our journey; rather, it was a sort of staging post from whence to head south in the hope of reaching Yugoslavia, no easy job, bearing in mind we had no maps. We had long since passed the last village our route markers had led us to, which had proved to be reasonably safe, as our builder friends had promised. We had seen Brno from one of the heights we had passed over and were now traversing the hills and valleys in between, using the sun by day and the North star by night. There were days when we could see no bright sky because of clouds which also denied us the stars at night. When we hit a road, the signs were no real help with their unpronounceable names! However, we kept on optimistically, hoping to be in something like the right direction.

I well remember that one evening our route had taken us through a wooded area bordered by cornfields when we came across an apparently empty house on the edge of the trees. Thinking it made a good landmark, my two friends decided to set off on a tour of exploration. I decided to remain behind. After hiding their packs under a pile of leaves, they set off. My position was pretty secure, lying down resting on the edge of the wood and listening to the sound of a piano accordion coming from a village in the valley. Evening was drawing on, and the sound of music was obviously coming from a dance.

The day was Saturday, and my thoughts turned first to England where similar gatherings would be taking place, and then to the war which had now spread from Europe to Russia, and for what? It seemed incredible that one man could have brought it all about, but such was the case and millions were now involuntarily embroiled in the mesh of fighting. The very country we were traversing now had been sacrificed to Hitler three years ago in a forlorn effort at appeasement. Instead of peace, Czechoslovakia with its armaments had only made war more certain by strengthening that maniac. By some freak of fate here I was, resting and enjoying the distant music this fine summer evening within a few miles of Brno, whose armament works were no doubt working flat out to feed the terrific appetite of the most powerful army the world had ever seen. Instead of fighting Hitler, the Czechs and most of the European would-be neutrals, because of Europe's bungling ideas of pacifism and Russia's treachery in Poland, were helping him, albeit involuntarily!

I awoke from my musings with a start to find my companions had returned from their fruitless exploration. After they had collected their packs, we moved off on our original route. We had not gone far before we came to the railway again. Alongside it were some allotments with vegetables in varying states of readiness. The sight of carrots took our eye and giving way to temptation, we set about sampling them. We were doing very nicely. The carrots, though small, were very tasty and made quite a change to our diet. To avoid being seen from the nearby railway, we were all lying flat on the ground, pulling and scraping them with our knives and devouring them at quite a fair rate. The carrots were disappearing fast, when, glancing to one side, I saw a pair of boots with feet in them supporting a pair of legs. Following them upwards I saw they belonged to an old man who looked as though he was ready to explode. He let out a burst of what was without doubt verbal abuse completely unintelligible to us, which was maybe as well! Quickly springing to our feet, we tried to calm him by offering him money, but to no avail. He continued his ranting. Seeing nothing short of gagging would quieten him, we did what came naturally; we took to our heels. When at last we thought we were at a safe distance we stopped for breath and had a good laugh.

The district we then made our way through must have been given over to market gardens. Further on was a miniature railway with boxes of garden produce stacked alongside ready for loading. Needless to say, we found helping ourselves easier in this vicinity than in the previous one. The principal 'samples' that found their way into our pockets were tomatoes and plums. Further on in distance and time, we passed an apple orchard which looked safe for a visit. We had hardly started when we were spotted and chased. Where on earth our pursuers had come from at that time of night completely bewildered us, but we did not stop to enquire. Once again that evening we took flight. Fear of capture must have given our legs speed, for we managed to escape.

By now we were into the outskirts of Brno and had no option but to continue on through the town. Sleep would have to wait till we were clear of the place and back in our 'natural environment', the open country. The streets were empty and silent but for our footsteps which echoed from the walls of the buildings as we trudged on in search of a safe place south of the city where we might rest up. We had to keep out of step to avoid any form of marching and vary the length of our strides, which was not easy. We tried to maintain the semblance of shift workers going on or off duty. What talking we did was in undertones. Our precautions seemed a bit ludicrous in the empty streets of that sleeping city, but we had cause to be thankful before the night was out.

It must have been between three and four in the morning when we suspected we were being followed. Whether we had heard an extra echo behind us and seen a dark shadow trailing us, I do not know, but we had got ourselves into a cul-de-sac, up a stone stairway, when we were challenged by a uniformed figure. We stopped and awaited his approach and then saw that he was a policeman in a uniform similar to the one our bobbies wore at home, but with a different type of helmet very like the old pre-war postman's helmet; in fact, rather like our police helmets with the top cut flat.

As he approached closer I spoke to him in German and he replied with the question I had anticipated, 'Where are you going?' My reply did not seem to surprise him; 'We're coming off shift work.' Then he turned his attention to our packs which I said contained in the main towels and soap for cleaning up at work. To confirm this he rummaged half-heartedly in one of our packs and found nothing to contradict my story. Fortunately for us, the market garden plunder we had accumulated was in our pockets, simply because it had been easier to fill them than take our packs off. He did not keep us long before he let us move on, much to our surprise; indeed we were flabbergasted. We had all thought that this encounter would be the end of our little adventure.

Somehow or other we found our way out of the cul-de-sac. Continuing through the night, hardly daring to speak to one another, when we did say anything, it was always the same question, 'Why had he let us go?' Our conclusion was one of three. He had guessed our real identity and, being a Czech, had turned a blind eye; he was a Czech with no better German than me and took us for Germans; or he thought the odds of three to one were too big. Of the three we were certain that the first theory was the most likely. Whatever it was, after the shock of being stopped, when our spirits had dropped to zero, they now rose to unbounded heights. Could it be an omen of final success? Our confidence increased a hundred-fold, and certainly put a spring in our step as we walked through the night and into the dawn, passing on our way a large factory complex that we thought might have been an armaments works; maybe the famous Skoda plant, where the Bren gun had originated? It was situated in a well-wooded, rocky area. The thought ran through our heads; what an opportunity for sabotage had we been trained as saboteurs! However, we all agreed we were not, so we came back to earth and our real aim; to get home and resume the job we had left in 1940.

Feeling on top of the world after our night's escapade and after resting up in a wooded hide-out into the afternoon, I took my partners into a beer garden in the first village we came to. Leaving them in the garden I went into the pub to get the ale, paying for it with a 20-mark note. I thought I had hit another snag when I saw the difficulty the landlady had in handling such an apparently large note. Her search for change involved the bar till and some vases at the back of the counter, but she eventually made it. I returned to my thirsty mates with two glasses in one hand and one in the other which also held the change, a few coins and a handful of notes, Czech of course. Some time after, fortified with the ale and a rest, we resumed our journey, passing a baker's shop from which came the wonderful aroma of fresh bread. I was sent off to try my luck again. As before, I was informed that bread was rationed and without the necessary coupons the bakeress could not sell me any. She did, however, cut a hefty portion off a large loaf and give it to me, refusing to take any money for it.

Thanking her as best I could, I rejoined the others and we continued on our way until we were well clear of all houses, when we camped in the vicinity of some heavily laden bramble bushes and enjoyed a meal of bread and brambles.

With something more substantial than ale inside us we set off again and after a few more miles came to what appeared to be a solitary house in the distance on the forest path. As we got closer to it we could see that, far from being one house on its own, we were entering a village complete with children and dogs, always a hazard for strangers who wanted to be unobtrusive. Both could be inquisitive and noisy. The weather was changing and rain was imminent by the time we were clear of the village. Night was coming on as was our tiredness after a night and a day on the march with only a brief rest period, so we looked for a billet. The best we could find was an orchard of plum trees, under one of which we settled to try and sleep, rain or no rain. Cold and wet, we huddled together for warmth. The sleep we found was fitful but not restful. The night was pitch-black. Discomfort overcame my attempts at sleep, and finding I was alone I stood up to stretch my legs. It was not long before I heard a rustling nearby and, more by touch than sight, found my two companions. Like myself they had got up, unable to sleep, and were passing the time till it became light enough to resume our trek in plucking and eating the luscious fruit. I was soon doing the same.

With the improving light we moved on, thankful for the warmth that the exercise gave us. We had eaten to saturation point and then filled our pockets for future consumption with the sweet-tasting plums. We were now looking for somewhere dry to continue our sleep. We were fortunate in our search, coming across a farm that was more modern than any we had previously seen. It had a large asbestos and steel barn half filled with baled straw stacked high enough for us to get out of sight of the farm workers, provided they didn't climb the bales. We soon made ourselves comfortable and dropped off to a more restful sleep.

When I woke up, the other two were already awake and alert to voices below us. Carefully avoiding being seen, we had a peep at the activity going on below. The odd worker or two came in from time to time, as also did a little white wire-haired fox terrier, but we were not spotted. Outside, the rain was still coming down as heavily as ever, and we needed no coaxing to staying there for another day in the hope of an improvement in the weather. What with the plums we had eaten during the early hours and the ones in our pockets we had consumed by now, we were forced to relieve ourselves very close to our 'bed-chamber', much to our sensory discomfort! This new self-inflicted nuisance we managed to put up with till early the following morning, when reluctantly we left these comfortable surroundings.

The rain had stopped and the sky was blue again, and we were in high spirits after our good rest, as we took to the trail again. Here and there we passed roadside shrines, a common feature in Roman Catholic countries. Further on we saw, lower down the valley, a building that looked like a monastery. Reflecting on our activities afterwards, I wondered why none of us had thought of trying there for help? Maybe we had imagined at the time that it might have been used by the Germans for billeting; after all, my squadron of the 'Skins' had been quartered in such a building in France. We were making good headway anyhow, and had the fortune to find a real haystack for our quarters that night, the first we had encountered up till then. On the way we had filled up with maize, which was both pleasant to the palate and kind to our stomachs that had suffered so much with the plums.

Being now clear of Brno, our next move was to seek out the railway again, having lost touch by moving south across country. Nearby was a church, a very picturesque little building, but the hour being early, we saw no human activity. There were no other buildings of any description in the direction we were going, only crops standing ready to be cut and fields that had been harvested. It was a glorious morning as we set off en-route for Austria. We were hungry, having finished our meagre store of rations, but we were in good spirits. By early afternoon, having covered a fair distance since leaving our friendly stack, we saw, a mile or so in front of us, what appeared to be a factory. We reasoned that by its size, some sort of railway might connect to it. Drawing closer and skirting it, we found what we were looking for, a branch line. This must lead us to the main line, so we made our way along the track until we could see a small town ahead.

Leaving the track, we continued along the road which now ran more or less parallel to it. By this time we were obviously in the outskirts of the town, and it was not long before we were on a level crossing. We were halfway across when we saw a patrolling sentry on the other side. As one man, we instinctively turned about and retraced our steps, without a word being uttered. Luckily the sentry had not noticed our action. In having a good laugh about our antics, we realised how stupid we had been in doing an about turn in the face of the enemy. The very fact that we had acted in unison showed the nervous tension we were being subjected to. One way or another we made ourselves scarce without being too conspicuous and did not return to the railway until the light was fading. Recognising the wagons as identical to those we had known at Morgenroth, again being shaped like the gable-end of a house, I was certain that they were destined for Italy. If we could hitch a ride in one we really would be making progress.

With this in mind how were we to conceal ourselves? We had two alternatives: in among the coal or in the brake cabin that each wagon had at one end. As was the usual practice, the coal was whitewashed as a means of showing if it had been disturbed in transit. To get among it without leaving telltale gaps in the white-wash was virtually impossible, so it had to be the brake cab. These had a door at either side, which were usually left open. Boarding one of these wagons, we crouched down inside the little lobby and left both doors ajar. Within half an hour or so we were on the move, and, although apprehensive, we were nevertheless elated at having achieved our original objective, a lift on a train.

Chapter 16

Railway

After about a couple of hours, the train stopped in what must have been marshalling yards, lit up as in peacetime, unfortunately for us. Had there been a blackout we might have fared better, but this part of Europe was out of reach of the bombers from England, and the Russians were too busy trying to stem the German advance to use their bombers for this sort of target. We heard German voices and guessed that some sort of wagon check was going on, and it was not long before we were found by railway workers. The police were soon on the scene. Complete with hand-cuffs, the three of us, me in the middle, were marched off to the railway traffic office. My rucksack, being slung on one shoulder only, was continually slipping down to the annoyance of myself and my friend on that side, whose arm had to rise with mine whenever I tried to get the offending bag back into position on my shoulder.

At the office we were frisked for arms, then were marched through the sleeping town to the police station and there searched again. From there we were taken to the local lock-up, where we were unceremoniously pushed into separate cells which seemed to be already full of civilian offenders. My accommodation was big enough to hold three beds and a wooden tub which served as a latrine. Two of the beds were pushed together under one of the barred windows, and the other was against the end wall. The five occupants of the two beds made room for me somehow; the single bed already had its full quota of three.

My new acquaintances, both Austrians and Czechs, were in for petty offences. They spent most of the time taking turns to keep a look-out through the bars for, strange as it may seem, the welcome entry into this jail of the Gestapo, provided they were unaccompanied by a prisoner. It seemed that this sort of visit meant the release of one or more of the inmates! Being minor offenders they were only short-term prisoners. What bit of food was dished up for us was the usual diet of potatoes, bread and soup. We had half an hour's exercise in the morning and again in the afternoon. Our other form of physical jerks was the daily routine of emptying the latrine. We were on a rota system and in pairs for this duty. I made friends with a Czech who was a sort of privileged prisoner in that his wife visited him several times a week. He was not in my cell but I met him on exercise and wangled a place next to him in the circle as we walked round and round the yard. He arranged to change the Czech money I had back into German currency with the aid of his wife. This transfer of cash we had to do as we walked round, but we managed it quite easily.

The company in my cell changed almost daily. One of our newcomers claimed to be a Hungarian who had just got back from Spain, to which country he had helped a Captain Anderson of Manchester to escape. He was confident he could get me there too, though for his services he would want a hundred pounds. The problem would be to make contact with each other when we left Lundenberg, where we were presently. For myself I was sure we would be returned to Lamsdorf when the German authorities got our escort organised, and my new friend was just as certain that he could contact me there. I assured him that that would be impossible and another venue must be found outside the camp. I could only think of my old job at the coalmine, and I assured him I would try to get there as soon as possible.

We spent nearly a week in this 'clink', and then on the arrival of an escort, we were on the move again. We travelled passenger train. Although we had only one guard, we had reason to believe we were under surveillance all the time. Any break-away would have dire results. On the train I did manage a bit of conversation with one of the passengers whose overcoat, I had noticed, had a Montague Burton label in it. He told me he had bought it in Newcastle, where he had sailed before the war as a seaman.

Our destination that day was Krems on the Danube, supposedly a French camp, but we saw very few of that nationality there, the predominant number of prisoners being Yugoslavs. We were housed in the camp prison. This was empty, and we had full run of the place. We were issued with a variety of French uniforms in place of our civilian clothes. These ill-fitting and shoddy garments gave us a bizarre appearance. Our only contact with the main camp was when we drew our rations, in a bucket. It was not the normal soup on issue in previous camps, a liquid that if run through a sieve would hardly have left any residue. The soup they issued to us was really a thick stew, and the quantity, bearing in mind that we collected it in a bucket, was such that we were putting on weight daily.

These Yugoslavs really looked after us; I almost think they thought we were supermen! Their admiration of England and the English was really incredible. Any conversation with these Balkan troops was very limited as we were always accompanied by an English-speaking German. In spite of our being so tightly chaperoned, they made strenuous efforts to shake hands with us. Their uniforms in a mauve-coloured woollen material struck me as having the best-quality cloth of any of the armies at war.

We were joined after a couple of days by another 'guest'. He was, we thought, a Russian, and in a terrible state of emaciation, as though he had lived rough for weeks and without food for most of that time. He was completely overwhelmed when we gave him a liberal helping of our stew, which we could see he had great difficulty in eating.

A day or two later we were on the move from Krems, where, we were told, Richard the Lionheart had been a prisoner at the time of the Crusades. We were, at last, on our way back to Silesia, via Vienna. On our arrival in the capital city we had to walk to another station, the West Bahnhof. During this hike I fiddled with my collar in an effort to get a note in German out of its hiding place in case we had a chance to get a drink of beer; the guard seemed friendly. In the large waiting room at the station was a motley crowd of people undergoing search by a couple of plain-clothes Gestapo helped by one or two uniformed Party members. The search did not apply to us, so I hinted to the guard that a beer would be welcome and proffered my money. Knowing we were secure, with the search party on the one hand and military police in prominence on the station, he left us to join a queue for the limited refreshment available. We saw the queue disperse and the shutters come down on the bar shortly afterwards and guessed the worst: sold out! So it was, and he rejoined us, as disappointed as we were. He returned my money and explained why there was no beer, although we already knew.

We soon forgot our disappointment as we watched, fascinated, the activities of the searchers. They were concentrating their attention on the travellers' luggage. Suitcases, boxes, bags and all the paraphernalia of containers used by their victims were ruthlessly opened and upended, spewing their contents on to the floor to be poked around in, prodded at and now and then picked up for closer scrutiny. All the while the examiners were almost contemptuously unconcerned with the anxiety of the owners of these goods who could only look on helplessly. When anything that might be termed contraband was discovered, the owner and the searcher would disappear into one of the side rooms. Shortly afterwards the searcher would return, alone. Those whose luggage had passed examination were left to repack as best they could. Their task was not made any easier by the partial destruction of the wrapping material in the course of being opened.

Such was the tyranny of the Third Reich, and what the war was all about. This was the way ordinary citizens were handled; but it was the result of Europe being too weak to nip Nazi tyranny in the bud. We, as merely interested bystanders, under *Wehrmacht* (German Army) escort, were spared this unpleasantness, but nevertheless eyes were cast in our direction several times. Thankfully we had not long to wait for our connection. We were not altogether without apprehension until we had boarded our train.

We were in a compartment of a corridor train where, already seated, was a young German woman. It was not long before our escort struck up a conversation with the buxom lass. It was easy to see he was a real lady-killer and never lost an opportunity of striking up an acquaintance with any likely member of the opposite sex. He was carrying a briefcase with him, not filled with our documentation, as we had thought at first, but with his victuals, bread and sausage. Having last eaten the day before, to say we were peckish would be no exaggeration, and we watched that case like hawks, always hoping that the unconsumed parts of its contents might come our way at the end of the journey. Alas, such was not to be, however generous he might have proved to be, because on the last train we boarded he got so engrossed with his amorous activities he forgot his case. To our dismay we did not notice its loss until it was too late to warn him.

After a fairly long walk from the station to the camp, we were back to where we had started a month or so before. Although we were hungry we were not dispirited. We had got some experience of the outside world which might be of some help in the future. We were also looking forward to some accumulated Red Cross parcels. As the hour was late when we got back, we were put in the 'bunker', the camp jail, for the night. Interrogation would follow the next day, and sure enough it did.

The following morning we were marched to the commandant's office, having only had a drink of that wretched liquid the Germans called mint tea, a tasteless drink that was used more for shaving or washing clothes than as a beverage. We were questioned as to why we had tried to escape; although we were interviewed separately, we had a well-rehearsed story about the poor working conditions on E211, the railway party. Our joint answers paid off; instead of the usual thirty days, we got away with twenty in the 'bunker' as the camp prison was nick-named.

The punishment was solitary confinement except for two daily exercise periods of half an hour. Our food was cut down to bread and water for two days, with normal rations on the third. Talking on exercise was forbidden. This was the only time we saw the other bad lads, and it was easy to tell who had been in the longest by their sallow complexions. Part of the exercises were in the form of *Hinlegen* (press-ups), not the easiest of pastimes on a meagre diet. After a day or two we had a new inmate join us, a real 'tough guy', who tried to defy the guards while we performed this exercise. They immediately stopped us and allowed us to take a turn at watching. They had a sense of humour: the 'smart Alec' who'd been smirking at our efforts became the source of our amusement, and by the time he was allowed to stop he had hardly the strength to stand up.

Chapter 17

Return

The time in jail passed slowly. As a means of whiling some of it away, I worked out the balance still due on our house mortgage; quite an involved mathematical exercise. Another rather gruesome pastime was watching the Russian dead carts leaving their camp which was not so far away. These vehicles, reminiscent of the covered wagons of Western films, but without the hoods, were to be seen, morning and evening, making their way to the cemetery. There were generally two of them with their loads of naked bodies, with arms and legs hanging over the sides. The Soviet Union was not a signatory to the Geneva Convention with its rules for making war somewhat more humane. Accordingly, where the Russians were concerned, the Germans had virtually no rules. This was reflected in the treatment of Soviet prisoners of war. As the war progressed the Germans in Russian hands suffered the same inhuman treatment.

Our conditions were pretty grim but nothing like those of both sides' prisoners taken on the Eastern Front. The Japanese were even worse in their handling of prisoners of war, as they considered them to be cowards, regardless of the circumstances of their capture. In contrast, we in German hands had a lot to be thankful for.

The guard commanding the 'bunker' was a disciplinarian and stuck rigidly to the rules, no more, no less; he was hard but not a sadist. When our time was up, we returned to the main camp, and I went back to where I was before our little expedition. Before I left, I had let Bob Hoe have my British overcoat and taken his tatty French one, knowing I would be leaving it on the working party when we left on our adventure. However, he had traded it in for a new one when a consignment of British uniforms had arrived at Lamsdorf and been distributed.

While we had been away, Red Cross parcels had been arriving pretty regularly. Our anticipated backlog, however, turned out to be a fancy. We knew we were being fiddled by our own administration personnel, but there was nothing we could do about it. In my own experience, the Germans were far more honest with these parcels and their distribution than were our own people, who had managed to get themselves into some sort of staff job in which to sit the war out. It took nearly a year before the general running of a British camp, as far as internal discipline and administration were concerned, was left to the captives themselves, with overall security the privilege of the captors. Any maladministration of Red Cross parcels thus became the problem of the internees – there was quite a bit of this going on.

The first period of captivity for the main body of British prisoners was after Dunkirk. For upwards of a year most of the victims of this debacle suffered captivity and the brutality of their victory-drunk captors in ignorance of the Geneva Convention. Those who started their prisoner of war life in hospital were for the most part fortunate in their conditions, but in reality they were not officially POWs until they left hospital and were registered and given a number. Until then the Germans were not accountable for them. Human nature being what it is, atrocities did occur. Prisoners were shot attempting to escape or whatever. This excuse for losses was as good as any. A lot depended on the guards, as I had already experienced on the mining party, where my position became not only untenable when the new guard took over, but even positively dangerous.

Another condition in the Convention that took nearly a year for us to find out was that only ordinary ranks were obliged to work. When this became known, a new type of non-commissioned officer was created, the Stalag corporal, as I have previously mentioned. Internal work in the camp was in a different category and much sought after for whatever perks it gave access to; consequently these jobs were hard to come by and for the most part were run by cliques. These could be regimental cliques, or a group from a common locality at home, or perhaps from one barrack or hut.

The top jobs in the camp were the prerogative of the senior warrant officers, who in my experience lived like lords, as did the cooks, for obvious reasons! Most of these fortunates settled down in their niches to sit out the war, and depending on their rank, await a healthy bank balance at home with their accumulating pay. On the other side of the coin were the trouble makers, who kept their captors on constant alert by organising or taking part in escape; or by indulging in a thousand and one acts of sabotage, mostly trivial but nevertheless having the effect of putting sand in the works of the Germans' well-oiled war machine. All these activities were frowned on by our own 'powers that be', especially the escapers.

Most prisoners of war acccepted stoically, and sometimes even with a certain amount of enthusiasm, the inconveniences brought on by others' efforts to leave; but those seeking a quiet life were not disposed to view these activities so philosophically, nor were they prepared in any way to help. Others rebelled against captivity in a variety of ways, not all of which were without risk. There were the wizards of the wireless, who contrived to produce news bulletins from the outside world in detailed reports, assisted by shorthand writers and home-made copying machines; such reports were circulated round the whole camp, as in my last camp, Stalag 383 at Hohenfels in Bavaria, but that was a year later, 1942. . . .

When our twenty days were up in the 'bunker', we returned to the main camp and the lifestyle we had such high hopes of leaving seven weeks previously. Things were now made more bearable by the comparatively regular delivery of the mail and the monthly clothing parcels from home. These were supposed to contain small articles of clothing, socks, scarves, handkerchiefs and the like; soap and chocolate could be included. (This was not a good combination as the soap affected the taste of the chocolate, and in my case I knew very well that my mother was depriving herself of that luxury, not having any connections on the 'black market'.) All the same, I looked forward to it, soap flavoured or not!

Chapter 18

Lorry

My billet was now in another hut, and I formed a friendship with Sergeant Phillips who hailed from Reading. He had managed to get himself a job on the camp lorry and shared his perks with me. He utterly detested the crowd he worked with, but stuck the job partly for what bits and pieces came his way, but mainly in defiance of the rest of the gang. Our life style was not much more than an existence, although I had found another interest, portrait sketching, putting into use some of the tips I had picked up from the French artist in the sickbay at Hemer. I had enough success in my efforts to have no real difficulty in getting sitters. My paper I bought on the camp market for a few fags, and later on had some sent from home.

As the new year wore on, my friend Phillips came more and more to detest the company he had to work with on the lorry and in the end he decided to give the job up. He offered me the chance to take his place. Although I appreciated well enough his reasons and knew what I would be up against, I took the job. For one thing I did not want our little perks to finish; more importantly I wanted to get to know the lay-out of the area round the camp. What better way was there than on the back of a lorry?

The first hurdle was to stand up to the resentment of the rest of that gang. I had crossed swords with the Germans in hospital, in Malines, and in the mine, so I was not going to be cowed by a bunch of back street gangsters from one of our larger cities! Their attitude to me eventually changed when I made them realise we had a common enemy in our present circumstances, and our efforts should be concentrated in that direction, and not against each other. In any case I was stuck with them and they were certainly going to be stuck with me, come what may. They got the message and although I never trusted them nor gave them chance to catch me out, our joint working improved.

We only travelled a short distance from the camp, and with a guard on the back our activities were very limited, but all the same we did not do too badly. In the course of our work, we went to the garage where the camp commandant's car was kept. On both front mudguards two swastika pennants flew proudly. What prompted me I do not know; maybe it was the sight of that hated emblem flying unmolested within easy reach. Unseen by anyone, I removed one and secreted it in my tunic, although not without some difficulty, as it was mounted on some stiff cardboard-like material. Stripping it down when I had the first opportunity on my bunk, I disposed of the stiffener and sewed one side of it behind my stripes and gave the other away. There must have been a lot of people who had access to that garage, because I never heard any mention of its loss, to my great surprise.

Our duties on the lorry took us to the Russian camp about a mile away. In Stalag VI A at Hemer, I thought I had seen men brought down to the lowest possible level that man could get to, in the conditions then prevailing in that camp; but compared to what the Russians were subjected to, we had been in the Ritz! The poor devils were doing their best to survive and many were not succeeding, as witness the dead carts, morning and evening, shifting their daily loads to the cemetery. It was hard to believe that these cadaverous objects, dressed in a multitude of rags in their efforts to keep warm, were once Russian soldiers. Their garb was stuffed with straw or grass, and they slouched about as though it took all their bodily strength to stay on their feet, let alone walk. Among them was a sprinkling of well-dressed individuals in good uniforms and overcoats, the camp police, also Russian. They were armed with truncheons or pickaxe handles, which they did not hesitate to use whenever they had an excuse for doing so. As far as we could tell, the main body of these prisoners were living in holes they had dug in the ground. The Germans had insufficient accommodation for the influx of so many prisoners captured in the initial stages of their Russian campaign.

We only went once or twice to that camp after that visit, and then only to the outer compound, no doubt to prevent us seeing too much and also as a precaution against disease. In such conditions it was not surprising that typhus, a disease endemic to filth, reared its ugly head.

The German authorities were terrified that it might spread to our camp, and we also had our fears. As a preventive precaution, we were ordered to shave every hair off our bodies and in spite of lack of facilities, particularly hot water, we carried out this instruction as quickly as possible. The reason behind it was that lice were the carriers of the disease. A cartoonist would have had a field day with material galore supplied by our antics as men in all attitudes struggled with blunt razors and cold water to remove the offending hair from all sorts of awkward places. While this instruction, which came from our own medical staff as well as from the Germans, was not obeyed with enthusiasm, it was carried out, more in self-preservation than in any other spirit. The amount of itching it engendered afterwards would have given a casual observer the impression that we were all as lousy as coots. As an additional precaution, all compounds were isolated with closed entrance gates, and food was left outside them. In one of the store sheds was a grim reminder – rows of black German coffins – of possible consequences if an outbreak of this dreaded disease should occur.

I do not remember any actual casualties, but there were two deaths which were an indirect product of the precautionary measures taken. Two new inmates arrived one night and were given newly de-loused blankets, only to be found dead in their bunks the following morning. Their blankets had been fumigated with cyanide gas and were issued before being well aired.

While the panic was on, our excursions on the lorry were somewhat curtailed, but we did make a few trips to the railway to load turnips for the camp, and in the course of our duties we managed to appropriate some for home consumption. We even got the guard to let the driver into our compound to off-load our spoils! By this time the quarantine arrangements had been called off. Another time we went for a load of bread in a French-made Ford van, which was really built as a troop carrier. In the course of loading we managed to secrete several loaves inside the mudguards. Putting them in position had not been a difficult job, but retrieving them nearly had us beat. We chased that van all over the place for our loaves and eventually succeeded in retrieving them, travel-stained with mud but otherwise none the worse, nor any less edible, after the mud had been scraped off them. We were nearly exhausted after the chase, but happy to have averted a tragedy; it would have been a disaster if that truck had returned to the garage with its contraband. After all, if they had been found, doubts about our honesty would have been raised in our captors' mind.

Another hair-raising episode in my career as a lorry-man came when three of us and a guard were shifting some crates of German army meat. With the guard on the back with us, the problem was how to breach the crates without detection. As it happened, the guard seemed to be deep in thought and only turned round now and again to look in our direction. What was really needed was a warning when this occurred. We were pretty sure he did not understand English, but any sort of alarm delivered in the normal way would be a giveaway by its very intonation. If we were to sing the words there would be no way of knowing they were not part of the song; so a singer was detailed to give the warning or all clear, whichever was required. The method worked and we made a fair haul without detection. The lightened crate with the spar put back was one of the first to be unloaded and hidden among the sound ones.

In all my experiences of felonious activities in the Third Reich, I found that a good maxim was, 'moderation in quantity', by which I meant, don't be greedy, be satisfied with what you can safely carry! Never overdo it. We had a good example of overstretching the mark when we were working with a bigger gang. We were doing very well until one of them was greedy and took a chance, only to be spotted. We all had to jettison our ill-gotten gains behind some of the cases we had loaded into the wagon for someone else to have a bonanza at the wagon's destination. We went back empty-handed, but the culprit got his deserts in the 'bunker' and his record card would undoubtedly be marked. If he was lucky it would be lost in the bureaucratic mountain of documents the Germans kept, as mine had been when I was sent back from my mining job.

As the year wore on and the weather improved, my thoughts turned to the open road, that being the young man's fancy in those years behind the wire. I left my lorry job and my distasteful co-workers, who had tried so hard in the initial stages to dislodge me, without success. I was leaving all the perks behind when I would need them if I was to make another bid for freedom. I had made friends with two Hull chaps from the East Yorkshire Regiment, Edie Harris and Jim Andrews. Like me, they both had itchy feet, and we decided to get on a working party and play it by ear, if any opportunity occurred.

We were sent to Sudetenland to work for a local joiner. The work was planing strips of wood by passing them over a revolving cutter, the pressure on the cutter determining the amount of wood cut off in the process of planing. We guessed the end product was skis for the Russian Front, although no one told us. We did not last long on that job, but long enough to ruin many of those embryo skis with our heavy-handed approach to the work. We were then found another simpler bit of joinery to do, building a shed at the back of a fruit shop, but our efforts there were matched by the amount of fruit the proprietor gave us . . . nil. Our antics embarrassed the guard so much that he himself took on most of the job while we watched.

Once again our employment was changed and we went to work in a saw mill. We all had different jobs there; maybe the Germans were cottoning on to us. My work was helping to put tree trunks through a jigsaw. The trunk to be cut was lined up on rollers, one end to the saw. The sawyer then sighted along it and turned it so as to present it the best way to the saw. Two blades about four feet long were inserted with wooden spacers holding them apart so as to make the first cut on both sides, taking the minimum amount of wood off. The saw was then started and the tree pushed through far enough for a clamp on the roller at that end to be used to hold it as the rest went through the saw. The tree was then moved back and turned on to one of the cut sides. The two blades were removed and several blades inserted with spacers between them of the same thickness that the planks were to be after the second cut. When sufficient length had gone through for the clamp on the roller to take over, the same procedure took place until the cutting was finished, leaving the former tree, now in plank form, at the other side of the saw.

The drone of the saw made it difficult for me to stay awake as I kept an eye on the log passing through in front of me. Before long we were sent back to Lamsdorf working compound and then back to our own compound. We decided we needed more preparation before venturing out again.

Chapter 19

Defiance

Fortune favoured me on our return to the camp. How it came about I cannot remember, but I landed a job among the type of gear we would need on our next attempt. I was given work in the store where all the invalid parcels were handled. My job was to open them and stack the contents in their respective categories on shelves. Believing in the 'justice of our cause', and seeing that the warrant officer in charge was living in his Aladdin's Cave with his office and accommodation there, and with his own cronies in regular employment, I set about acquiring gear for our projected trip. Edie and Jim, meanwhile, had lost no time in starting the ball rolling. They had been trading with some Greeks, swopping spare khaki gear for civilian clothing, and managed to get enough for the three of us, bar one jacket.

Getting hold of some packing-case wood, I selected it for size and thinness and made two suitcase-type boxes. Both had false bottoms and lids covering about three-quarters of the box that tucked under the other quarter spar which was a fixture. A movable spar under this fixed top piece disguised another inch or so of hiding space, which together with a false bottom of about an inch, proved handy in concealing escape gear. A central dividing board completed the deception and served to baffle the eye. The lid became the side when the case was carried as a normal suitcase. It was held in place by protruding battens which tucked under the fixed portion of the lid; two buttons, one on either side, held the bottom. Handles of plaited string slotted into the top endpiece completed the job.

I tried to get what gear we needed legitimately by dropping

hints to the warrant officer in charge, but without success. He regarded would-be travellers as damn nuisances, who made life more difficult for the rest, including himself. He was typical of the type who, having got a good billet, were content to stick to it.

I had a quiet laugh to myself when a poor lad with one leg came to see the commanding officer. Whatever he had wanted, he had been refused. In place of his missing leg, he had a wooden effort shaped like the bottom of a crutch, and I made good use of it! Using adhesive plaster, I strapped it with tins of food, which his empty trouser leg hid. I wondered how he managed to walk with his load; not with a lightened step, maybe, but certainly with a smile on his face. I remained in this employment for a week or two until we were ready for our little expedition.

The change of clothing was secreted in the two cases, as were Horlicks tablets, glucose, oatmeal and chocolate. In with the gear we were legitimately supposed to have we had a tin or two of sardines and some chocolate, though not enough to raise any suspicion when any German official rummaged through the cases and rucksacks. Edie and I had a case each, and all three of us had a rucksack containing, for the most part, odds and ends of clothing that could be discarded later when the rucksacks were put to their intended use on the walk. After volunteering for work, we landed jobs in a brewery. Edie and I had left our 'stripes' with friends for safekeeping, also my souvenir pennant. We were moved over to the working party compound, preparatory to going out to work, and here we would remain, as was the usual practice, until our escort came to take us to our new-found employment.

While we were here an incident occurred that nearly ruined all our efforts. A general roll-call and search was on. We were paraded outside our quarters and lined up between them and the latrines for several hours while the billets were searched. All was quiet except for mumbled curses directed at our guards, two of whom stood between us and the latrines. They made it obvious that no one would be allowed to leave our ranks to make use of that building, when one of our number decided he could wait no longer and started to move in that direction.

Seeing this flagrant challenge to authority, one of the German soldiers unslung his rifle and held it at the ready, shouting in the full harshness of the Teutonic language, 'Halt'. The offending

POW ignored the order and in a demonstration of sheer guts continued in the forbidden direction. The atmosphere became indescribably tense, even more so when the guard rattled the bolt of his rifle, making it obvious to all that he had 'one up the spout'. By this time his companion had his rifle at the ready. As one man the whole mass of assembled prisoners, who had previously been sitting, squatting or lounging, as befitted their tiredness after their long wait, stood up and made their intention obvious. For seconds, that seemed like ages, the impasse remained. It only needed a pressure on the trigger of either of the guards' rifles, and they would have been torn to pieces: of that I had no doubt. By now the defiant prisoner, who had continued walking throughout these dramatic and tense moments as though oblivious to anything but the purpose he had in mind, had nearly reached his destination. At the very last moment the guards relented, and a murmur of relief went through our ranks. Soon more of us were making our way, in dribs and drabs, to the latrine, completely ignoring the guards.

Shortly after we were allowed back into our quarters to find our things in disarray but intact. Our cases survived the search, to our relief and my own satisfaction,. We had had the sense to leave them open with only sundry items of underclothing, books and so on in an untidy heap, half-in and half-out of the cases. The Germans were, for the most part, looking for wireless sets, maps and similar gear. In my own experience, the safest place was often in front of their eyes.

Chapter 20

Hansdorf

A few days later the three of us and a guard set off for Lamsdorf station. After a comparatively pleasant journey by passenger train lasting about three hours, we arrived at Hansdorf in Sudetenland. We appeared to be replacements for three who had gone back sick. I was greeted by one of the work party, who must have known me, with the hardly friendly remark, 'Hullo, what have you come for?' The accommodation was in a high, roomy building, with three-tier bunks, trestle tables and forms. There was one drawback; the usual sanitation for night use when we were locked in. The place was clean and the food slightly better than camp rations.

My job was in the large underground section of the brewery. Here the beer was stored in massive barrels, laid horizontally in two tiers. When the beer was drawn off, the large bung section was removed, and, armed with a candle on a spike, a brush and a hose pipe, I had to climb in and scrub the tarred interior ready for the next fill-up. With the candle spiked firmly to the side of the vat, I set about the job with some gusto. The cellar's natural temperature, summer and winter, was 2°C above freezing, hence my enthusiasm in scrubbing. Above ground it was a very warm summer, but below it was nearly as cold as a refrigerator.

During work I was frequently passed a large aluminium jug of ale which had been stood in a wooden bucket of hot water for long enough to take the edge off its temperature and so prevent possible stomach trouble. Drinking so much required an outlet, but it was not necessary to go far, with all the water that was continually leaving the vat through the bung section aperture. We were equipped with gum boots and overalls as protection against so much water.

In the short time I was at this brewery I did see a beer-taster testing the beer. On asking how strong it was, I was told it was seven per cent for civil use and fifteen per cent for the military. The only conclusion I came to with these figures was that the forces' beer was twice as strong as that in a *Gasthaus*. The questions I asked were intended purely as a hopeful opener to conversation, but without success; the taciturn taster was too busy testing for taste, sediment and colour, and then spitting his sample out.

Meanwhile Edie and Jim seemed to be having a variety of jobs, connected for the most part with the finished product. I was not particularly interested in the work we were doing, but rather in the business we had come for.

The brewery was alongside a main railway line, with trains passing through day and night. There was little opportunity for us, however, to find out enough about a possible lift by that route. As far as I could judge, we would have to make our way up the wooded slope behind the brewery and then head south till we were well clear of Hansdorf. We conferred in the evenings with comparative ease as we walked round the place. The guards were relaxed, and really, why not? What POW in his right mind would want to leave this heaven-sent haven for a refuge in war-torn Europe? The party had been there for over a year and had had no trouble at all in that time until we arrived on the scene, as it turned out. I can honestly say, such was our keenness, that none of us gave a thought to stopping there; neither had we any qualms about the rumpus we would create by our intended action.

We had decided on the date for our excursion, Sunday, 2 August 1942. It was a non-working day, which might give us a bit more time before we were missed. We had broken open the secret areas of our our cases without drawing attention to their concealed gear. The day being ideal for sun-bathing, we were in shorts and, wait for it, gum boots. We needed these to help us convey most of our gear which we were assembling secretly up the mountainside. Bit by bit we managed to get most of it out of our billet without arousing any interest. I even found time to have a yarn with one of the guards watching the rail traffic going past. A trainload of what appeared to be prisoners of war went by, with a guard in each wagon; their uniforms puzzled me, not being German, and their rifles were silver barrelled and not the usual blued steel. The guard told me they were Russian and so were the prisoners they were guarding, evidently defectors.

The bulk of our lads had been on some sort of hunt in the afternoon, which activity had without doubt helped us in shifting part of our gear up the mountain. The quarry they had been hunting was caught and killed and its skin hung on the washing line outside our accommodation – a snakeskin.

It seemed there was not a dull moment that afternoon, because, shortly after the snake hunt, we had a visitor from Lamsdorf, the camp commandant. Believe it or not, we had to wake the guards, a duty we performed with discretion. I was in the group who were entertaining this high personnage when the guard commanding officer appeared on the scene, red faced and apprehensive. I could not help wondering what our visitor would have done if he could have read our thoughts. Whether his visit had anything to do with it, I don't know, but our tea ration came just before his departure, and we received a chunk of bread and a reasonable piece of German sausage.

It was an ideal time for us to move and we did, still carrying our issue. We went like the clappers up that mountain side and changed into our civilian clothes that we had previously cached. We had already changed our footwear before leaving. We were just about ready to start off again when we heard rustling lower down the slope. Hardly daring to breathe, thinking we were being pursued, we crouched behind our cover, a thick clump of bushes. Then we heard voices, to our surprise in English. We must have been 'tumbled to'; possibly the welcome we had had on joining the party had resulted in others cottoning on to the idea. We kept in hiding and several fellow members of our party passed near to us, some still carrying their tea ration, but without showing any signs that they knew we were there. Had we set the fashion, in spite of our efforts at secrecy, or was this already planned?

All in all, I had some feeling of guilt. Had we not upset a really good place of employment, where twenty-four prisoners of war could have waited for the war to end in comfort? On the other hand, were we not still soldiers with a duty to break loose whenever possible? Whatever the risk we took, our break had not resulted in wild shooting involving others, neither had we solicited help from civilians, thereby risking their necks and those of their families – though we might have done so had the opportunity arisen.

The idea had entered my mind in the early days, when I was in Brussels, along with the story of Nurse Cavell. I had some qualms about the fate of the guards. After all, they had been a decent lot who had turned a blind eye on some of our antics, as, for instance, when we appropriated one or two crates of bottled beer and took them into our quarters. We had to take a crate as it would not be missed, whereas odd bottles would have been noticed by the gaps in the crate. We always understood that guards who 'lost' prisoners would be sent to the front. All these thoughts ran through my mind while we waited to give the other 'runners' time to get well clear before we started to move. All this long pause was filled with the fear of pursuit, particularly if the others had been seen on our route.

COMPETITION MAKES A LAST-MINUTE RUSH NECESSARY AND AFTER WORKING ALL DAY, WE ARE, AT LAST READY. A PHOTO IS TAKEN AND WE MUST MOVE OFF – 9:30. WEDNESDAY 25TH AUGUST 1943. WALKING IN THE SEMI-DARKNESS WE ARRIVE AT 1ST GATE AND ARE NEARLY 'SUNK' BY SOME ORDERLIES ASKING US TO TAKE THEM TO HOSPITAL!

WITH 'NIX' 'MOSS WARTEN' WE 'STAVE THEM OFF' AND OUR PAPERS BEING O-K WE MOVE ON TO THE MAINGATE, SUMMON A 'POSTERN!' AND GO THROUGH SAME PROCEDURE SUCCESSFULLY.

WE WALK THROUGH, SAYING 'GUT NACHT'.

NO SOONER ARE WE OUT, WHEN THE LIGHTS GO OUT AROUND THE CAMP, AND WE MUST WALK IN FULL GLARE OF THE SEARCH-LIGHTS COVERING ROAD AND WIRE! PASSING THE GUARD BILLETS WE SEE THE WHOLE 'WACHE' TURN OUT – FOR THE CAMP ALARM!

NOTE: ANOTHER ESCAPE WAS BEING ATTEMPTED VIA THE WIRE, AND THE LIGHTS WERE FUSED JUST AS WE GOT OUT – HENCE THE USE OF THE SEARCH-LIGHTS AND THE GUARD TURN OUT.

CAMP PAPERS, NOT NEEDED NOW, ARE
DESTROYED – THE GASTHAUS OR CANTEEN IS
PASSED AND THEN WE DISARM, AFTER PUTTING
CONTENTS (SANDWICHES) INTO OTHER
POCKETS!

CROSSING FROM ONE ROAD TO ANOTHER, WE ARE QUESTIONED BY A STRANGER BUT SATISFY HIM WITH 'WARM NICHT WAHR?!' WE REACH THE ROAD AND CARRY ON, MEETING SOME 'SIGNALS' LAYING A TELEPHONE, WHO SHINE A LIGHT ON US BUT SAY NOTHING. BY ABOUT 2 A.M. WE HAVE REACHED PARSBERG AND DECIDE TO WAIT FOR DAY, IN A WOOD.

I SLEEP WHILE MY PAL COUNTS THE TRAINS. RISING AT 5:30 A.M. WE CHANGE, BURYING AND DESTROYING THE FIELD GRAY (GREEN!). WE ENJOY A CIGARETTE AND PROCEED TO THE STATION. WE ARRIVE AT THE STATION AT ABOUT 6 A.M. AND TRY TO MAKE OURSELFS INCONSPICUOUS.

AFTER 5 OR 10 MINUTES WE OBTAIN TICKETS TO
NÜRNBERG. SEEING A PLAIN-CLOTHES-MAN ON THE
PLATFORM, WE TAKE THE FIRST TRAIN THAT COMES
AND FIND OURSELVES ON THE WAY TO
REGENSBURG. THERE WE TAKE THE TRAIN TO
NÜRNBERG. HAVE BIT OF TROUBLE RE-TICKETS,
WITH CONDUCTRESS, BUT 'GET AWAY' WITH IT!

*WE PASS THE BARRIER AT NÜRNBERG
WITHOUT TROUBLE, AND MY PAL TRIES TO
GET TICKETS FOR CRAILSHEIM WHILE I
'DODGE ABOUT' THE STATION. AFTER A HALF
HOUR WAIT HE 'TURNS UP' WITH WRONG
TICKETS – BUT TRAIN IS GONE IN ANY CASE!
SO WE TAKE A WALK TO THINK THINGS OUT.*

NEAR THE STATION, ITSELF DAMAGED, WE
SEE RESULTS OF AIR-WAR! A NICE LITTLE
'PUB' OFFERS ITSELF TO US, SO WE ENTER.
MY PAL ALARMS ME A BIT WITH HIS 'PROSIT'.
LEAVING THE PUB WE RETURN TO THE
'BAHNHOF'.

A CHANGE OF ROUTE IS DISCUSSED
AND ONCE MORE WE 'TRY' FOR
TICKETS. THESE BEING OBTAINED,
FOR HEILBRÖNN (AS WE THINK!), WE
GO FOR ANOTHER WALK, BUY PAPERS
IN STREET, AND CARRY ON. CINEMAS
ARE THOUGHT TOO DANGEROUS,
BECAUSE OF POLICE NEAR QUEUES!
RETURNING TO STATION, WE HAVE
DRINK IN RESTAURANT.

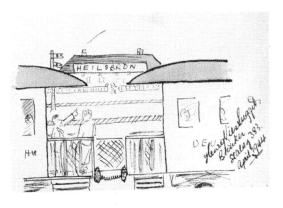

HAVING DIFFUCULTY
EATING SANDWICH
BECAUSE OF TOO MUCH
MEAT IN IT! MY PAL BUYS
LOTTERY TICKETS WITH NO
LUCK, WHILE I AM
INTERESTED IN ITALIANS AT
NEXT TABLE. WE CATCH
TRAIN AT 2.16 PM. WE
REACH HEILSBRÖN IN
30 ODD MINUTES!
REALISING SOMETHING IS
WRONG, WE INQUIRE FOR
STUTTGART TRAIN AND ARE
TOLD WE'VE JUST LEFT IT!
WE ASK FOR TICKETS – ARE
REFUSED – NO TIME, AND
TRAIN GOES.

THINKING IT TOO DANGEROUS TO HANG AROUND WE MOVE ON. MY PAL ASKS FOR DRINK AT FARM AND IS TOLD 'YOU'RE FOREIGNERS!'. I REPLY 'YES, BELGIANS'. WE GET DRINK AND MOVE ON. WE LEAVE THE PATH AND FOLLOW THE LINE.

IT IS VERY WARM, IN BLANKET SUITS! RAILWAY WORKER IS INQUISITIVE AND I TELL HIM WE ARE BELGIANS (INTERPOSING A WORD OR TWO OF 'PIDGIN' FRENCH TO MY PAL) AND HAVE LEFT TRAIN BY MISTAKE SO ARE WALKING TO NEXT STATION TO PASS TIME AWAY WHILE AWAITING THE NEXT TRAIN. HE DIRECTS US AND IN 10 MINUTES WE ARE THERE. A 'LICK' AND A DRINK AND HAVING SEEN OUR MISTAKE (HEILBRÖNN AND HEILSBRÖN!) MY PAL BUYS TICKETS TO STUTTGART. HE HAS DIFFICULTY WITH DIALECT!

A PLEASANT HOUR OR SO IS
PASSED IN WINKLESGREUTH
STATION RESTAURANT, UNTIL –
THE ENTRY OF A COUPLE OF
'COPS' CAUSES US TO RETIRE TO A
PLATFORM SEAT. WE LOOK AT
TICKETS – HAND WRITTEN – AND
THEY SEEM OK – BUT!!!!
THE TRAIN COMES AND WE BOARD
IT.

THE WORD ANSBACH WRITTEN ON THE TICKETS MAKES US THINK WE CHANGE THERE! WE LEAVE THE TRAIN AND LOOKING AT TIMETABLES IN THE SUBWAY WE REALIZE OUR ERROR AND RUN BACK, IN TIME TO BOARD TRAIN, IN A DIFFERENT COMPARTMENT.

NOTE: TICKETS WERE ONLY MADE OUT FOR ONE. ONE WAS ORDINARY CHARGE AND OTHER EXPRESS SURCHARGE!

AFTER HOUR OR SO'S JOURNEY WE HAVE TO LEAVE TRAIN, AS WE ARE APPARENTLY AT THE TERMINUS! DOMBÜHL! NOT FANCYING THE WAIT FOR STUTTGART TRAIN WE BOARD TRAIN FOR CRAILSHEIM, WITHOUT TICKETS! TROUBLE RE-TICKETS (A MAN DRESSED AS FORESTER SEEMS INTERESTED TO MY HORROR!). WE ARE TAKEN TO STATION MASTER (IN RED HAT) AT NÖROLINGEN WHERE CONDUCTRESS TRIES TO EXPLAIN THINGS. ONCE AGAIN WE ARE BELGIANS WITH SUCCESS AND AFTER BUYING MORE TICKETS TO DOMBÜHL PLUS FINES WE ARE 'PUT ON' TRAIN AND IN THE CARE OF CONDUCTRESS, BY CONDUCTRESS OF PREVIOUS TRAIN!

AT DOMBÜHL THE CONDUCTRESS GETS US TICKETS FOR STUTTGART AND AFTER A WHILE, WE GET ON BOARD THE EXPRESS! IT IS CROWDED MORE WITH AUSTRIAN TROOPS THAN CIVILIANS AND WE FIND PLACE IN JOINING BETWEEN 1ST AND 3RD COMPARTMENTS IN MIDST OF SOLDIERS AND THEIR BAGGAGE! AFTER ABOUT COUPLE OF HOURS, AT ABOUT 11.30, I AM SUDDENLY ASKED BY A PLAIN-CLOTHES-MAN, IF I AM A CIVILIAN OR A SOLDIER. TELLING HIM THE FORMER, HE ASKS FOR PAPERS AND WE MOVE INTO 1ST COMPARTMENT BECAUSE OF LIGHT AND NEAR MY PAL. PAPERS AND STORY NOT BEING 'IN ORDER' WE GET ORDERS TO 'KOMM MIT'.

WE ANNOUNCE WE ARE ENGLANDER FELDWEBELS TO THE SURPRISE OF SOLDIERS AND ARE TAKEN TO POLICE COMPARTMENT WHERE WE SEE OUR 'OLD FRIEND' THE CONDUCTRESS OF THE PARSBERG TRAIN. WE HAVE A CHAT WITH ANOTHER (AN OLDER) P.C. MAN (AFTER HE HAS LOADED GUN!) A BLACK (VERY) MARIA TAKES US TO THE BIG HOUSE.

AFTER COUPLE OF DAYS WE ARE SENT TO STALAG VA, FLÜCHTLINGES ABTEILUNG WHERE WE MEET SIMILAR MINDED FRENCH, BELGIAN, POLISH, SERB AND DUTCH (SAILORS) PRISONERS. A CONCERT IS ORGANISED ON QUEEN WILHEMINA'S BIRTHDAY, AND MY PAL SINGS A SONG OR TWO! AT CLOSE ALL ANTHEMS ARE SUNG AND WE TWO PLUS NEW ZEALAND PAL SING 'THE KING!' WE FINALLY ARRIVE BACK AT CAMP AND BUNKER!

Chapter 21

Escape and Recapture

Setting off again we veered to the left of our original direction, hoping to avoid following in the steps of the others. Our general aim was south. We had no map to go by, only our memory of the geography of Europe. On our way, when we had cleared the forest and were travelling in open country, Edie robbed a scarecrow of its hat, and I managed to get a jacket. It was not long before the trilby was put to another use.

We had gone a few miles and were resting in the sunshine on the fringe of the wood, when Jim gave me a dig in the ribs. At first I thought something was wrong. 'What's up?' I asked. 'Look over there,' he replied, pointing to a spot just inside the wood. Following his directions, I saw Edie on his hands and knees collecting something, and every now and then putting something in his mouth and then carrying on depositing whatever he was collecting in his hat. Moving closer, I saw what were the objects of his attention; wild strawberries, no bigger than peas. He carried on devouring them as though his life depended on them. Jim and I had a good laugh, but that did not upset our imperturbable companion.

On the whole this expedition was a repetition of my previous venture. The terrain was similar except that we seemed to encounter more water obstacles, which took a lot of time to circumnavigate and did not help us to find our direction. Neither did the weather favour us. There was far more rain than the previous year, and in consequence, more cloudy skies and sunless days followed by starless nights. As before, I acted as scout, making trips into the villages and pubs.

On one of these expeditions I ventured into a little pub and sat opposite the bar with my beer, while a joiner was mending a hinge on a door. The living quarters were behind the bar and the landlady was preparing lunch for her children, the time being nearly midday. The aroma issuing from the kitchen was both an appetiser and a torture! The joiner meanwhile had finished his job and was paid, as far as I could see, in the currency of POWs, cigarettes. By the time she had finished with the tradesman, the sound of children's voices indicated their arrival home from school. The clang of an oven door and resultant tantalising odours confirmed this.

Soon after, I rejoined my pals, and we set off on our long march. This day was one of the few sunny ones, and we interspersed our hike with rest periods to catch up on sleep and also to dry our clothes. That evening found us still heading across country. As darkness fell, it being a clear night, we could steer by the stars – the Plough and the North star. This was alright until we came to a thick wood, which cut off our view of the sky and stars. Progress was virtually impossible, but my companions thought differently and so we entered in single file, trying to maintain our course.

On we went again, thinking we had corrected our navigational errors, only to find at the next clearing that we seemed to be going in a circle. Continuing again, back on course as it seemed, we eventually found ourselves out of the trees and more or less back to our original starting point. This was verified by a landmark we had passed on entering, an old stack near the wood on open ground. We finished up doing what we should have done at the start, lying up for the night.

We were on the move pretty early the next morning and, coming across a field drain with running water, we shaved and smartened ourselves up. A few hundred yards away was a main road on higher ground than the field. As we neared it we saw some of the locals evidently going to work. We cut our pace down a bit in order to let them get ahead of us and, in an effort to make myself look a bit tidier in my old jacket, I put my hands in my pockets to keep it swept back. Everything was alright till we had to mount the slope to get on to the road, when I slipped and fell flat on my face. As my hands were in my pockets, I could not use them to break my fall. My nose took the full force and bled profusely.

Fortunately the passers-by took only a cursory glance in our direction.

By now we had been out a week, making a bee-line across country, living off the land and our own meagre rations, which included a wet mash of oatmeal and cold water, since we did not dare to light a fire. Shortly afterwards we encountered the railway again, to our relief.

On the evening of the eighth day we found what we hoped would be a source of a lift, a sort of small freight-yard. Up to now our freedom had been comparatively uneventful, and that had possibly lulled us into a false sense of security and complacency. Whatever it was, we were completely taken by surprise when an 'old fogey' in German uniform challenged us with levelled rifle and marched us to a signal box nearby. As we walked along the railway line, we could not help discussing how easy it would be for us to overpower this old fellow with his antiquated rifle, but where would that get us when the hue and cry went up? We would be easily picked up, and then what? Unlike the heroes of many escape yarns, we never contemplated resorting to violence, unless it would have been expedient, say on the frontier with Switzerland. Nevertheless the old man would have been scared if he had understood our remark, 'We could do the old boy in, if we wanted.'

Once in the signal box, more help was summoned over the telephone, and shortly afterwards the police arrived and escorted us to their headquarters, where we were questioned and finger printed. Edie, with a bit of manoeuvring, disguised the fact that he had the tip of one finger missing! From there we were taken to a small building with barred windows, some sort of a lock-up. A series of boards battened together and mounted on trestles served as a bed.

We still had our rucksacks and the remainder of our rations. After a bit of a nap, we took stock of our surroundings. The building we were in was at the corner of two streets, and by standing on the trestles we could look out of the barred windows. In the world outside very little was happening, as it was early Sunday morning and not really late enough for the little town to come alive. However, we did manage to buy a newspaper through the bars. The town was Muglitz, according to the paper which was in German, and the full front page was about the hammering

Hull had received from the German Luftwaffe. The date was 9 August 1942. The news was not exactly designed to cheer us up, what with the numbers of raids, casualty figures and value of damage, and percentage of houses rendered unfit or completely destroyed. Since the war, in my various terms of office as Mayor of Hedon, I have mentioned this coincidence to several of the Lord Mayors of Hull, in the hope that one or other of them, using the facilities at their disposal, would try and get a copy of this newspaper. It was a strange experience for the three of us to get hold of news in such circumstances, and to see our home town receive such publicity from the enemy, when back in Britain reports referred only to a northeast coastal town.

As the day wore on, we still received no attention, being apparently left to our own devices. We consequently decided to help ourselves. The door was like an ordinary batten door, with a hasp and padlock on the outer side. We used Edie's trilby on the end of one of the trestles to minimise the noise while we used the trestle as a battering ram and with one blow we had the door open. The padlock had come adrift and to get it out of sight I put it down a flue in the corner of the building.

Venturing out into the open area at the back, we found a pump, which we put to good use, having a wash and quenching our thirst. While we were at this, a woman with a child in a push-chair passed by. Seeing us, she went white with fear and rushed past us as quickly as she could go. It appeared one of our trio had been looking out through the bars when she had passed earlier on. By reason of an exclamation she made, we assumed she thought we were Russians! German propaganda had always asserted that Russians were fierce barbarians.

Soon after that the police re-appeared and held an inquest on the spot as to how we had got out. They thought that the woman from whom we had traded the paper had tipped off the local resistance, who had let us loose. We told them the true story, which they did not believe at first. The missing lock puzzled them, and so, rather than let them blame the paper seller, we disclosed its whereabouts. Even then they refused to believe us. To check our story they sent for a chimney sweep, who, after a lot of probing and soot, produced the offending article.

In their relief at solving this serious crime they rewarded us with some food. I was picked to go with a policeman to a local café. There they prepared three hot meals and stacked them up, one on top of the other, with those metal rings used for that purpose. We were just ready to set off when the bobby reminded them that it was a meatless day. This was a method of rationing meat in Germany at that time. The plates were separated and the meat removed, to my dismay! We were then marched off to the main police station and, after the customary search, were put in separate cells, containing the usual minor offenders who were daily awaiting release. In anticipation of this they kept a look-out at the windows. The second day there saw the entry of a soldier and that heralded our next move.

Our return journey was uneventful. On being interrogated at Lamsdorf as to our reason for leaving the brewery, we all had the same story of atrocious conditions in that party. Our story must have been swallowed, because our punishment period was only five days. Little did they know, apparently, of the disruption we had caused at Hansdorf. Had their bureaucracy been remotely efficient, we would have been sent to a *Strafelager*, a punishment camp, for possibly a year. Fortunately for us, it seemed that all they had to go on was our report; though it was possible that some of the other wanderers from that party had already passed through their hands and made the same excuses.

The normal Stalag jail was full, and we were put in a make-shift one, an ordinary barracks partitioned into cells. In the centre of the floor was the by now familiar wooden tub. A rota was kept, detailing two men whose job it was to empty this unsavoury object each day. Because there were something like a dozen names in front of our three, and we were only serving five days, we knew we would be out before our time came.

This fact upset the guard commander, and he stormed into Edie's cell next to mine, cursing in German and accusing both of us of dodging the column. Standing on my bunk I could see over the partition wall separating the two cells. The only support I could give Edie was more abuse in my best Silesian German, which had the effect of diverting his attention to me. Rushing out of Edie's cell, he charged into mine, bayonet in hand. The air was filled with shouted imprecations and he got redder and redder in the face, flourishing his bayonet like a Roman gladiator. The argument nearly got to the pushing stage, which could have been fatal for me if I had allowed temper to beat me. He was only waiting for an excuse to use his weapon. Edie was adding his voice to the rumpus, which shortly after ended abruptly, when I think my adversary, possibly realising he had gone too far in letting his temper get the better of him, turned on his heels and left, muttering to himself.

That was the nearest I had come to disaster. I have always had an aversion to bullies, not just the physical type, but also those to whom a bit of power goes to the head. On comparing notes with Edie, when we were back in the main camp, we found we both had the same fear, when confronted by the infuriated guard, over standing our ground, but also another and greater fear of being seen to chicken out.

While in the 'bunker' we had heard rumours of the start of the 'Second Front', which in reality turned out to be the debacle of the Dieppe Raid. The aftermath of that ill-fated expedition was the tying up of prisoners in retaliation for the bodies of Germans found with hands tied on the beaches after the raid. The real explanation was that it was a precaution taken by the raiders, who wanted prisoners complete with papers and insignia intact. Unfortunately, some of these had been killed while on their way to captivity along with their captors.

As far as we knew, the Germans' retaliatory action was first started at Lamsdorf. In the beginning a thick band was used to tie the victim's wrists across his front. It was kept on from 9 a.m. till 9 p.m. Troops from the nearby rest and training area were used for the job both of tying up and of ensuring that we remained tied. They were all armed with sub-machine 'Tommy guns'. As time went on the thick band disappeared and string from the Red Cross parcels used in its place. Later on, both these materials were replaced by handcuffs, specially made for the job. The two cuffs were joined together by a short chain, allowing more movement of the arms and hands. They were quite easy to open with a knife or nail. In the beginning the tying up was very rigidly supervised by the Germans brought in for the job. They numbered those whose Russian Front experiences had made them nearly inhuman, and those who had been made more human once they were away from that inferno.

Shortly after coming out of jail, I found myself with a batch of non-commissioned officers destined for an NCOs' non-working camp. such at least was the rumour, and for once the rumour was right. The Geneva Convention was at last being honoured. After a lengthy journey by train, in true POW fashion forty to a wagon, we arrived at Parsberg, a little village halfway between Nürnberg and Regensburg. Our final destination was a former camp for Yugoslav officers, about ten miles from the station.

Chapter 22

Hohenfels

Hohenfels, the little village from which the camp derived its name, was an apt description of the area, the English interpretation being High Rocks. The terrain was hilly, with large woods and open ground intermingled, and in parts outcrops of rocks and crags. The camp was in the centre of a military training area. The main accommodation was in rows of wooden huts, each designed to hold sixteen bunks, arranged in four pairs, each two tiers high, down either side. In the centre of the camp were several larger buildings, including the camp theatre and one or two others that later became a sports building, a school and a store for Red Cross parcels, as well as a more substantial structure, the cookhouse. In an inner enclave, wired off from the main area, were several utility buildings, German offices, the camp post office, coal store and bread store. Outside the main camp were the administration offices and the camp hospital. On one side of the area was a large sports field, approached through large gates from inside the camp, which was wired off from the main enclave. Situated at regular intervals round the perimeter were watch towers manned day and night, armed with machine-guns and searchlights. The camp prison was well clear of the perimeter and had its own wired surround.

Our quarters were well-built wooden huts about sixteen feet by twenty-five feet. The solitary door by which one entered off the camp road had a window next to it, and at the other end were a further two windows. For heating each hut had an upright stove from which a pipe led through the roof, serving as a chimney. A trestle table with a form either side completed the furniture. A large aluminium bowl and jug served to collect our rations. The bunks were the standard wooden two-tier type; a lath running the full length of each side supported the regulation seven bed boards.

Before our arrival the camp had held Yugoslav officers. It now held British non-commissioned officers and warrant officers who under international agreement could not be forced to work. Most of us had been in captivity for two years before this fact came to light. In our early days in that camp the discipline was fairly strict, but after a few months it gradually relaxed, almost to the point where we were running it. We were divided into a dozen companies by the areas we were living in, and the morning roll call was by companies. To facilitate the count we were always lined up in fives. It was the common belief that this was the only way the Germans could count. Indeed, on several occasions when we were short of a man or two, we delayed discovery for a day or so by means of shuffling around the rear files.

The tying up of our hands, that had started in Lamsdorf, was continued here with the issuing of handcuffs. Each morning a detail of guards came round our billets with these barbaric objects. The whole business became a complete farce, with the chain bearers fitting them on us in the beginning, followed by our taking the bracelets off after their departure. In the end they gave up and would come into the hut enquiring, 'Wievel?' – 'how many?' – and leave the requisite number on a nail behind the door. Later, these same guards became traders and salesmen, taking orders one day and bringing the required goods the following day. Currency being of little value, barter became the means of payment.

It was nothing unusual to see the German who had brought the sixteen pairs of cuffs disgorging his wares from his pockets with the extreme care needed with eggs, unbuttoning his tunic to get at the frying pan with its handle stuck down his trousers, and then pull a vital part for a wireless out of one of his pockets. In an attempt to curb our illegal activities, the powers that be had patrols strolling round the camp day and night and entering huts at will. These patrols for the most part worked in pairs and were mainly of the rank of *Unteroffiziere* (corporals). They inevitably had some success now and again, and we were sure that their booty found its way back into the camp a short while after. In modern idiom, it was recycled.

Apart from the daily roll calls, every now and again a full muster of the entire camp would be held on the sports field. On these occasions we were checked by our identity photos. This was a long-winded affair and upsetting to the normal running of the camp.

Gradually we got ourselves organised, and sports, theatricals and concerts, of orchestral dance or brass band music were given in one of the bigger sheds that had been converted into a theatre. Enterprising individuals started little businesses in the front of their huts, borrowing one of the forms and setting it out like a shop with a variety of articles for exchange or sale, the price marked up in the POW currency of cigarettes. Others set up gambling games, with cards, dice or even pennies as in the Australians' national favourite, two up.

This game was at first played in the open air, with the gamblers forming a ring round the thrower, who took up position in the centre with a flat piece of wood on which were placed the pennies, three being the norm. His stake, invariably a packet of ten fags on the ground, was 'covered' by anyone in the ring. The thrower would then launch the coins into the air, in the hope that two or more would show heads when they landed. If tails were in the majority, he was declared a loser and retired to the ring of bystanders. If he won, he threw again, his stake now being doubled. This was repeated and if fortune favoured him, he would then have, after three wins, a stake of eight packets. After three successful throws, he had the option of retiring with his loot, which was now seven packets, the organisers having taken one packet for their work. On the other hand, he could continue and throw again if he so chose. This time he had to throw two winners before he could draw and, should he be successful, he would now have twenty-seven packets after the organisers had claimed their fee. From that point on throws were singles, and he could take whatever he desired out of his winnings, but the 'table' took one after every successful throw. This game was played on improvised tables, both in the open air and in the huts, but instead of pennies, dice were used, specially made with H and T markings instead of numbers.

Another popular gambling stall had cards and a stand as big as a card table. This was faz, where only the top five cards in each suit were used, along with the joker. These were shuffled by any of the players or onlookers and the top card removed still face down. The four deuces were lined face up in a row, one below the other, and the remaining twenty cards, still face down, were placed in the four rows thus formed, each with a deuce at the top to denote the suit. When all bets had been placed, the game started with the croupier turning the single card over and moving it to the place occupied by a face-down card which in turn went to the row and place in the row denoted by its suit and value. The card occupying that place was removed to lead to the next, and so the game continued. Every card that was turned over was a winner and paid evens. Bets could be placed on multiples of the cards in a variety of ways: all the aces, all the kings, and so on. All of each suit, all the corners and even the joker could be backed to be the single starter card. In that event all bets are void except the one on the joker which would qualify for odds of twenty to one.

Both these gambling games are very fair and, in the case of two up, can produce some fantastic wins. The biggest I ever saw was a throw of twelve heads consecutively, which resulted in a win of approximately 1800 to one. This was on a 'table' made of floor sections from one of the huts. The winner had been drawing out on the way. As the stakes increased with every throw, so did the crowd round the table, which included several Germans, incredulously watching the drama.

The reader may wonder how a win like this was possible with our Red Cross allocation of fifty cigarettes with each parcel. These were intended to arrive in quantities sufficient for an issue of one per week per head. However, parcels came in fits and starts, and any gaps in between were not automatically filled. Prisoners whose relatives were 'well breached' – rich – received fags by the thousand, but they were in the minority. Private fag parcels were a very welcome addition, even if they sometimes affected the market. Heavy smokers would sell part of their food parcels for the weed. As time went on, we reached a point where cigarettes were traded and bought through credits via the paymaster, the going rate being £15 per thousand.

I cannot remember the circumstances under which I changed my billet, but I found myself the only British prisoner in a hut full of Australians. They were a mixed lot, a commercial traveller, a student, several farmers and a firewood dealer (who called himself a timber merchant). All had one thing in common; they were all volunteers. I found them very friendly and amiable, but not against a bit of pommy bashing! This was good humoured, and I had no difficulty in holding my own, more so when I acquired a smattering of their lingo and became a cobber, 'stone the crows!'

After a month or two we were joined by a couple of Palestinian Jews, sergeants in the Palestine Labour Corps. Although they were Jewish, they were wearing British uniforms and consequently were treated the same as the rest of us. It was an irony of fate that the elder of the two had been an officer in the Austrian Army in the First World War, but was now on the opposite side. He was a very tough old boy and regularly took a cold shower, regardless of the weather, as soon as he got up in the morning, although this entailed a walk of fifty-odd yards to the wash-house, very often through snow or mud, clad only in his greatcoat and a towel. His companion was considerably younger and a brilliant musician, as later he was able to demonstrate when we eventually got a piano in the camp. Rumour had it that this came about when the commandant, a lover of good music himself, learned of his ability.

It was round about this time, in the first few months of the British occupation of the camp, that I found myself mixing with like-minded inmates with 'itchy feet', who had sampled the fresh air outside the wire. In the course of comparing notes I had been shown a copy of an *Ausweis*, that is, an identity card. I thought it shouted out aloud its lack of authenticity. I could only think of one way to back up my criticism and that was to make a better one.

One thing led to another and I built up a connection with Sergeant McCallam, who became the head of the camp escape committee. I was able to help with a bit of forging now and again. One of the most frequent little jobs I did was putting an official stamp on passes. In doing this comparatively simple art work, I was always given access to the appropriate stamp for the job. These were masterpieces of carved wood which, when smeared with a copying ink pencil and damped and pressed on to the forged passes, completed the effect. There were two types of pass, those issued by the army and those by the police. As a rule the town of issue, which occupied the centre of the bottom circular dotted line, was left to me to fill in.

There were other jobs of a more urgent nature. Civilians, generally old men, working on a camp job would shed their jackets in warm weather. If it was considered reasonably safe, their wallets would be borrowed and a copy made of any passes that might be in them. I never knew who was responsible for borrowing them, but I had several of these jobs to execute.

Working in a safe hut and using a window as a vertical desk, I would hold the pass with my paper flat to the glass and without too much difficulty trace the lettering with a pencil. Voluntary runners kept contact with the scene of the borrowing, and if it became necessary, the wallet and pass could be returned before their loss was found out. The hardest part for me to do was the list of conditions on the back of these *Ausweise*, the wording being in very small Gothic print.

Whereas indelible pencil was the most suitable ink for fake rubber stamps, the passes themselves were done with a mapping pen and Indian ink and mostly on typewriter copying paper. Where any typewritten lettering was required, the camp office machine was used. Some of these passes carried a photograph of the bearer, as is the case with passports. In the beginning of our occupation of Hohenfels, cameras were not to be had, but as trading with the Germans developed so did camp photography, although it was officially forbidden.

The time-honoured method of exit, tunnelling, seemed to be going on all over the camp at one time, but by its very nature it was labour intensive as well as requiring almost limitless quantities of that scarce commodity, timber. Huge quantities of earth spoil had to be disposed of in such a way as not to be conspicuous. Hazards met en route included water pipes, electric cables and drains. Many a good project underground had to be abandoned when three parts completed through meeting up with one or other of these hazards.

Chapter 23

German Uniforms

The establishment of a camp school was another direct result of efforts to make life a bit more bearable. With the help of the Red Cross the more studious among us could, by studying, improve their chances when the war was over. Exams could be taken in this camp under the strict rules obtaining at home, and it was possible to work for degrees in almost any subject. Before the war I had worked for a small firm of fish merchants and pondered, in between my activities with the pen, on studying for a degree in economics. This entailed improving my French and German, maths and English, and of course studying economics.

Full of enthusiasm for my new project I enrolled for the course at our new school. Among the internees in most camps were experts in pretty nearly any subject under the sun. In my enthusiasm I had the promise of help with my German from the younger Jewish man in our hut, who had a native mastery of the language, as did his companion. He started me off by giving me 'Lorelei' to learn, which I did, mostly by the light of the searchlight in the nearest look-out. I still know it, unlike one or two other poems I learnt at the time. I was also attending the school for economics, which seemed to me to be an elaborate study of the basic laws of supply and demand and human behaviour, with a whole lot of variegated theories written into them. Nevertheless, I did not think it was beyond my comprehension, if I put my mind to it.

Whatever else came of my new interest, it made a change from the eternal problem of finding a way out. I had not abandoned escape, but this schooling made a break from what had almost become an obsession. I persevered for some weeks in my studies, which did not, however, stop me from making the odd *Ausweis* or two whenever asked. In this connection I was approached by Sergeant George Beeson of the Royal Electrical and Mechanical Engineers, who wanted two copies of the passes issued to the German NCOs who patrolled the camp, generally in pairs, and whose job was snooping. They wandered in and out of huts keeping their eyes open for anything unusual, wireless sets and signs of tunnelling being their main preoccupations.

I knew the only way these passes could be used would be by masquerading in German uniform, and this was precisely what my scheming acquaintance was planning. George had made friends with one of these snoopers, an Alsatian who had no loyalty to the uniform he was wearing, and who, for a 'consideration', was prepared to lend his pass for an hour or two. I had serious doubts about his genuineness, but George was certain that he was on the level. I made the required two copies, plus a spare for future reference, after the loan of the genuine pass two or three times. That, to all intents and purposes was the end of my commitment, or so I thought. George, however, had other ideas.

When he had first approached me, he had mentioned that he was leaving with a Spaniard, hence the two passes. I never gave it another thought until he told me his would-be confederate had changed his mind; would I like to take his place? I must have had an inkling of his ultimate intention, because my response was simply, 'Why not?'

The next job was to get our costumes. These were to be Australian tunics and battle-dress slacks. The only attention they needed before dyeing was the removal of the two outside pockets. George had already acquired a German side-hat, one worn on the side of the head, and sufficient tunic buttons. The belts I made out of cardboard, along with their holsters. The buckles I made of silver paper and the words 'Gott mit uns' I wrote with thick Indian ink, hoping the heavy shading would pass for the embossed lettering on the real buckles.

Setting about the hat, I started with the band, making a cardboard ring to fit my head. Allowance was made for some tightening up when it was covered. The cover itself consisted of a piece of material in the form of a sleeve turned inside out so as not to display the seam. The flat circular top was achieved by a piece of semi-stiff wire, with the loose ends finishing at the front and twisted to give enough rigidity when secured to the flat band in the center. In this way the front of the hat was held up. The round top was covered with a piece of khaki shirt, and four more pieces of khaki reached from the ring to the head-band with their seams vertical front, back and at the sides. A peak of boot-polished cardboard and chinstrap of the same material nearly completed the job. Buttons for the strap and a home-made badge were added. Some fiddling with the wire gave the hat a bit of a rake. It was quite a job and one that gave me some satisfaction. At the time it never occurred to me that in less than a year I would be making another! The markings round the edges of the shoulder straps and collar worn by *Unteroffiziere* were made with silver paper, and the swastika eagle worn on the right breast by the *Wehrmacht* was made out of a small piece of linen-like material.

An incident that could have had disastrous results for our projected expedition occurred when I was still working on the passes. As was the practice, I always had a look-out or two from among my room mates to warn me of the approach of any stooges. As I had done some work on the passes and put my gear away, my sentinels had withdrawn, when as if from nowhere a couple of German guards walked into the hut and set about searching the few of us inside at the time, before giving the hut the once-over. There were about six or seven of us in at the time, and I kept at the back of the queue, trying to think of a way to hide the damning evidence I had in my wallet. It was incriminating enough to get me sent to a *Straflager* and, even worse, to get our friendly Alsatian shot.

To try and get my bulky wallet out of my pocket and hide it in front of the two stooges would have been suicidal. In desperation I racked my brain for a way out, all the while watching my companions being searched. All of a sudden it struck me: they were being searched in shirt sleeves, it being a very hot sunny day. Very leisurely I took my tunic off and hung it on the end of a bunk, all the time trying not to show the rapid palpitation of my heart. In due course my turn came and I passed the examiner's search. I then ambled over to the bunk, slung my tunic over my shoulder and sauntered unhurriedly out of the hut, but bursting with my desire to run.

Once outside I made my way down the roadway, still at a snail's pace in case I was being watched, but, although I was tempted, I never turned round to see if I was being followed. All that time I was expecting a shout calling me back for my tunic to be searched. I went to a friend of mine, from the Yeomanry, Lance Sergeant Arthur Sellars. Not having a record, he was not so liable to be searched. Moreover, I had implicit trust in him. When I had unloaded my 'hot material' on him, I went back to my billet, in case my searcher had remembered not having checked my tunic. I was now without any incriminating material on me. By returning straight away I had given him the opportunity to complete his search there and then.

In the meanwhile George had been preparing to dye the uniforms, having got the dye from his co-operative *Unteroffizier* friend. So far things were progressing smoothly. My passes only needed the fictitious names of their holders to be typed in and they would be complete, a little matter that Sergeant McCallam, who had access to one of the camp machines, would see to, as commanding officer of the Camp Escape Committee. When this was done, there remained only the date stamp, which I would add when the day was finally decided. Our other passes, for use when we got out and began our travelling, I had already prepared. George assured me that the dyeing had been done and the costumes, laid out in the sun behind his hut, should be ready for the final bits and pieces to be sewn on the following day. A safe hut had been organised for us to do the final dressing up in. It was not too far from the first gate we would have to go through. Our gear was assembled in it, ready for the 'jump off' that evening, and I dated the passes, 25 August 1943. There was no going back on this date other than by making new passes. To add to the urgency, George, who always seemed to be tuned in to the grape-vine, came to me with an item of news that only served to stress the importance of our departure being earlier rather than later that evening: another escape of a very daring nature had been planned for that night. It was to be a raid on the perimeter fence, using ladders to scale the inner wire and planks to span the outer wire, with dummies to draw the fire from the watch towers. The whole attempt was to be eased by fusing the perimeter lights.

We with our little plot could have done with another day to make sure our uniforms were dry, but if we waited till after this escape bid all our efforts would have come to nought with the turmoil that would follow such an attempt. Resting as much as we could the following day, not an easy thing to do with all the excitement engendered by the double-feature evening 'programme', we were glad when sunset came.

We first donned our civilian clothes in the safe hut, and then our *Wehrmacht* uniforms. Our dressers helped us with the belts and holsters, sewing them at the back, as they had no real buckles at the front, only silver paper dummies. The holsters were packed with bully-beef sandwiches and one or two items of sustenance were stuffed into our pockets. The passes we each had in our left breast-pockets. While all this was going on, I suddenly remembered one of the camp amateur photographers had asked me a day or two before if I would tip him off when an escape was taking place in case he could get some form of photographic scoop. He was billeted nearby. I asked one of the helpers if he could contact him, which he did. The photographer promptly came back with his escort and camera.

Chapter 24

By Rail to Nuremberg

Using the old-fashioned method for poor light, our photographer posed us for a few seconds, took his photograph, thanked us and left. I never knew his name, but a few weeks after being brought back, I managed to get a couple of copies of that night's scoop. One of these I still have, the other I hid in a New Testament and asked a warrant officer who was repatriated in 1944 to send to my mother when he got back to England. This he never did, and from a letter I got when I managed to beat the repatriation queue just before the war ended, it was obvious that my courier had ditched his clandestine material.

Immediately the photographer had finished and left that evening of 25 August 1943, we set out for the unknown. So it seemed as we left the comparative security of the safe hut for the first hurdle, the inner gate, with our hearts in our mouths. Our masquerade passed its first test in a manner that could very easily have been our undoing. A couple of our Royal Army Medical Corps personnel approached us at the gate in the hope that we would escort them out to the camp sick bay, where they no doubt worked. In the best German we could muster we told them to be off, it was not our job, and walked past them. Whether or not they were ever told of our true identity we never knew, but our performance was good enough for the guard, who hardly looked at our passes, venturing a 'Gut' Nacht' as we walked past him. We then set off towards the main gate which was approximately one hundred yards away. I likened the walk to that of a condemned prisoner on the way to the gallows.

Excitement at our first successful encounter with near disaster and anticipation of the next and possibly greatest test of our ruse ran through my entire frame like an electric shock. I am sure George was feeling the same by the gist of his whispered conversation with me as we trudged on nearer and nearer to the big gate. As the distance diminished to the last twenty or so paces, we kept up a muttered chat in German for the benefit of the guard we had to pass. 'Hast du von deiner Frau gehört?', 'Wie geht's mit Heinrich?' and such like phrases passed between us until we were at our second testing point. The postern here was every bit as obliging as the first one had been, hardly looking at us or our passes and we soon found ourselves outside the camp. We then turned left to walk to the hospital as the guardhouse was on the other side of the road.

We had hardly gone a few yards when the camp was plunged into darkness – the other escape was on. In our preoccupation with our own break, we had forgotten about the other attempt timed for that night. A lot of shouting was going on, and as we passed the guardhouse its inmates were spilling out with a rattling of accoutrements and guttural ejaculations as they lined up to march to the scene of disturbance. George, with a cheeky grin, remarked, 'We should take charge of these bastards, we're *Unteroffiziere*', a suggestion I did not take him up on as we continued on our way, unnoticed as far as we knew.

The road to Parsberg, where we hoped to catch a train, meandered through hilly country freely littered with outcrops of rock. The gear we were wearing, uniforms and civilian suits under them, was far from ideal that hot August night. However, our elation at the success of the first part of our adventure more than made up for the physical discomfort. Our route took us past a *Wehrmacht* canteen with the usual sounds of revelry one associates with beer drinking and the occasional tinkle of a piano. The odd German or two passed us, as they tumbled out of the door to make their way back to their billets. A casual 'Gut' Nacht' sufficed for conversation as they staggered past us, as it did when we encountered groups of Germans on some form or other of night exercises. One particular group stands out in my memory; they were signals troops laying a field telephone with cycles festooned with coils of wire.

We eventually arrived at a little wood outside the station where we laid up after our walk of about ten miles. As the clock got round to nearly six the workers started to gather on the station and we decided to join them. By now we had discarded our uniforms and belts, burying them under heaps of leaves and rotting foliage. Our passes, which had got us out of the camp, were torn to shreds and scattered as we walked during the night. On the station nobody took any undue notice of us, all seeming too busy with their own affairs. George, who fancied his German better than mine, bought two tickets for Nuremberg.

While waiting for the train we had our first alarm. My fellow conspirator had spotted a man among the waiting crowd who, he was certain, was a Gestapo agent who had visited our camp during one of the searches. Thinking he might recognise either of us, we boarded the first train that came along, which was travelling to Regensburg, the opposite direction to where we had bought tickets for. We wandered through the various compartments to the end one which was like an observation carriage and I enjoyed a fag as well as the scenery, although the pleasure was somewhat diminished by the thought we might have to explain to a ticket inspector how we came to be on the wrong train. Little did we know we would be quite dab hands, before the day was out, at explaining how we came to be travelling with the wrong tickets.

All went well to Regensburg, where we got off without incident and boarded the right train this time. It was pretty well filled. The carriage we were in had seats facing each other on either side of a gangway down the centre. George and I sat facing two old lasses who were too busy chatting to each other to notice we were there, for which we were both thankful. All went well until we were almost back up the line to Parsberg, when we nearly had a fit; the conductress came round checking tickets. George being nearest, tried to explain how we came to have tickets bought at Parsberg when we had not yet reached that station. Whether or not she understood his explanation, she accepted his story without any fuss, to our great relief. The whole of Germany was swamped with foreign workers, and we supposed our little episode would be one of many that she had experienced.

On reaching Nuremberg, the first leg of our route, we studied the wall maps and timetables aiming at our second leg, Stuttgart. That involved too long a wait, but we could get a train for Heilbronn at 2 p.m. As that town was just north of Stuttgart, we thought it would be better to go there than hang about where we were. My partner joined the ticket queue, while I endeavoured to make myself as inconspicuous as possible to the Gestapo agents and Hitler Jugend members dotted pretty obviously about the station. When George was about to get to the ticket hatch it clamped down, and he joined the scramble for the next window. The resultant delay in being served did not help me with my dodging about. As it was, I must have been successful in my efforts because I was never challenged. I hustled George out of the station as quickly as I could when he joined me with the tickets.

Outside Nuremberg station itself showed a fair amount of bomb damage, and in the vicinity was evidence of the visits the city had had from the Royal Air Force, some of it quite recent. Whole sides of buildings had collapsed, leaving the interiors exposed like a child's doll's house. We had about an hour and a half to lose before we could catch our train, and seeing a queue for a cinema, we joined on, but not for long. A couple of policemen were interesting themselves in some of the public waiting to go in. Without a word, we left the group to which we had attached ourselves and set off back to the station. On the way we had to pass a pub. That was not so hard to do, but to broaden our experience we stopped for one. George had read a lot about German customs and glass clinking was one of them. Fortunately there were only two or three drinking and they were too engrossed with their own problems to pay much attention to my companion's theatrical gestures.

Back in the station we joined several other travellers sitting at a large circular table, occupying themselves in a variety of ways. Some were having their lunch, for the most part bread and wurst. One in particular was the proud possessor of a hard-boiled egg which he was shelling with hands gnarled by years of hard work, matched by his weather-beaten face. A young soldier busy writing a letter paused every now and then for thought or inspiration. Next to him were a couple of middle-aged workers eating their bread and wurst. The little gathering sat in complete silence, to our relief, not wanting to be drawn into conversation. Their whole demeanour was sombre in the extreme; it might even be described as miserable. The war was taking its toll of human misery and the strain of the prolonged conflict had certainly left its mark. What a difference to 1940, when Germany was cock a hoop with victory.

Taking a chance, I bought a couple of beers. By that I mean I risked another glass clinking with George. As it was, in following the crowd and eating our lunch we had to be careful not to expose the contents of our sandwiches. At a table nearby three or four men appeared to be in a heated argument, judging by their raised voices, but glancing round, I could see it was nothing worse than a game of cards. By their appearance and the sound of their language I took them for Italians.

While my gaze was directed to that side of the room, I spotted an old man in some sort of uniform, with a tray suspended by a strap round his neck, who was heading in our direction. His wares were lottery tickets, as a notice hung from his tray made plain. George had not seem him approach, being too interested in some of the other people around us. I managed to rouse him with my elbow in his ribs and muttered, 'For goodness sake, buy some,' which he did. The vendor took his money and selecting an envelope from the bundle on his tray, tore it open and took out a paper with a number on it which he then compared with a printed list he had; he muttered 'Klein Glück', and moved on to seek another victim. Both of us agreed that for once in our lifetimes we were pleased not to have won, given all the complications that winning might have brought about.

Shortly afterwards, fortified with the beer and bully in our bellies, we boarded our train. We were anticipating a journey of some two to three hours but within about half an hour the train had stopped. Our hopes were shattered by the name of our destination, a little country station called Heilsbronn.

Chapter 25

Heilsbron to Ansbach

Jumping off, we hurriedly crossed the lines to where the red-capped ticket collector-cum-station master waited. Something was wrong, it was obvious, but what? Acting as spokesman, I asked him, 'When is the next train for Stuttgart?' 'That's it,' he replied. 'We've made a mistake, we'd better get back on,' I retorted as we turned round to rejoin the train. 'You've no tickets.' 'We'll get them on it,' I replied, by which time the train was gathering speed, making re-boarding impossible. We turned back for the station and ignoring its one official, made our way to a country path that ran parallel with the rail track. We did not stop until we were well clear of our arrival point.

The afternoon was hot and so were we after our sprint across the rails in our blanket suits. After a while we reached a farm bordering on the iron way, where a group of workers were unloading a wagon. Nearby was a pump; on our asking for permission to use it, one of them muttered something about foreigners but they nodded approval. Rinsing our faces and with cupped hands managing to drink, we felt considerably more comfortable. Refreshed, we continued on our way, sometimes on a road and other times on a footpath, hugging the railway all the time. Further on we were questioned by a railwayman, but our explanation of how we came to be where we were, that we had got off the train by mistake, seemed to satisfy him. Three or four miles further on we came to the next station, no bigger than the last except in name, Winkelsreuth. Here George essayed to buy tickets again, this time for Stuttgart. These were hand written, and seeing we had two with the same destination on them, I never doubted that we were in possession of the correct ones this time. Had I done so it might have saved us some bother later on, but not wanting to cast any doubt on his knowledge of the language, I said nothing.

This station boasted a waiting-cum-refreshment room to which we retired to await another train. We consoled ourselves with a couple of beers in the welcome shade, glad to be out of the sun, and pondered over our predicament. We were correct in our conclusion that there must be two stations with very similar names.

After about twenty minutes our tranquillity was shattered by the entry of two policemen. Finishing our beer we wandered on to the platform where we found a seat. Shortly after we had settled down a train came in. We found it was going to Ansbach, a name on one of our tickets, so we boarded it, and soon were mobile again. After about an hour we arrived at a station bearing that name. Thinking we might have to change there, we got off and consulted a wall map we found in a connecting tunnel between platforms. In the light of this new information, we decided to get back on the train, which fortunately had not yet left. After about another hour's ride we reached Dombühl, where everybody got off except us. It was not long before the conductress told us too, to get off, that evidently being the terminus for that train. Not wanting to draw attention to ourselves, we did as instructed. In our efforts to maintain a low profile among the mass of humanity we boarded another train, this time to Crailsheim.

All went well until we were asked for our tickets, which of course were not in order. The conductress took us for foreign workers, fortunately for us, and made herself very helpful. At the next stop, I think it was Nördlingen, she took us off the train to the general office and, as far as I could make out, explained that we were trying to get to Stuttgart and had got ourselves lost. Our hand-written tickets, bought at Winkelsreuth, were for one person alone, and not one each. The second of the two was some sort of surcharge for travel on an express. Some express, I thought, but said nothing to George about his prowess at purchasing tickets. My own command of the tongue left a lot to be desired, but at least, being a Yorkshire man and from Hull, I had a far better accent for that guttural language. George came from the south of England. The outcome was the purchase of two tickets to Stuttgart and the payment of some sort of fine for our free travel. Luckily we were not short of money. Our helpful escort put us on the right train and instructed the conductress of that train to make sure we got off at Dombühl, to await the connection that had proved so elusive all day.

Here we had quite some time to wait before its arrival, which must have been around 9 p.m. Whether or not anybody else boarded it I cannot recollect, but the compartment we got into was brimful of German or Austrian mountain troops; so full indeed that we finished up over the coupling between two coaches, with men and equipment filling the corridor. The adjoining compartment must have been first class, because now and again officers came to the toilet near where we were. We were literally rubbing shoulders with German mountain troops complete with eidelweiss cap badges and steel-shod boots. Their caps were similar in shape to those worn by the Afrika Korps, except for the colour, field grey. I was really fascinated by our situation; two British prisoners of war mixing with Germans who could not have had the faintest suspicion of our identity, and on the wall of the coach, in full view of us all, the warning 'Feind hört mit' – 'the enemy is listening'. Neither of us dared to speak, for obvious reasons. George was lounging in the first class side of the join and I was actually on the steel plate joining the carriages. I was more incredulous than apprehensive at the chancy situation we now found ourselves in. We had started off wearing *Wehrmacht* uniforms, albeit home made and now twenty-four hours later we were in the middle of scores of wearers of the real gear. No particular attention was paid to us and we aroused neither curiosity nor interest from our travelling companions; nor did any of them make any attempt at conversation, fortunately for us.

Chapter 26

Captured

We must have been on that train an hour and a half before trouble arrived in the form of a portly, middle-aged German in civilian clothes who wanted to see our papers. George was slumped on the floor with his back to the carriage wall, a position he had assumed simply by letting his feet slide forward as sleep overtook him. I produced my Belgian worker's pass (a product of the ingenuity of someone on the Escape Committee, rather than a copy of the genuine article). The stout controller passed it over to his partner who had now joined him, and it was obvious to me that they were not impressed by the document, by the way they started to throw questions at me. By now George was fully awake and on his feet, but seemed to be content to leave the interrogation to me. Among the questions were, 'What address are you going to?', to which I replied, 'We don't know, our friends are meeting us on the station.' By now it was pretty obvious that lack of documents authorising changes of work place and accommodation had been our undoing, such was the tight grip on the populace, whether German or alien, that the state maintained. George had heard all that went on while feigning sleep and was not surprised when we were told to 'Komm' mit'. We were led into a compartment reserved for the *Krontrol*. On our way we spoke to each other in English for the benefit of the soldiers and announced our true identity: 'Engländer Soldaten Kreigsgefangenen'. The looks of amazement on their faces as we squeezed past them had to be seen to be believed. It would have made a good cartoon, of the type Bateman was famous for before the war.

The other occupants of the reserved compartment were our fat friend's assistant, a younger, slimmer person in the civilian disguise worn by so many of the Gestapo, a black leather coat; and a railway conductress, who could not take her eyes off us as we took a seat next to our captor. The atmosphere was remarkably good humoured and our 'friend', who was a game warden before the war, even went to the extent of showing us photos of himself in his former occupation. The woman opposite us was obviously trying to puzzle out something connected with us. Eventually she burst out, 'Du und du'. I still could not fathom her particular interest in us, although her face seemed familiar. 'What was all that about?' I asked George, and he soon gave me the answer: 'she had been on the first train we had boarded that morning and remembered the cock up we had made then. The time was nearly midnight, which meant she had been on duty for something like eighteen hours.

Shortly after we arrived at Stuttgart and were conveyed to the police headquarters in their equivalent of our 'Black Marias'. This vehicle was divided into individually partitioned seats with a central walkway. On our arrival we were searched and interrogated: 'Where did you get the *Ausweise*?' George replied that he had made them. A writing pad and pen and ink were provided for him to show his capability in writing in Gothic script, but although he could read that sort of print, he did not have a clue when it came to writing it. They did not bother to ask me. If they had, I would not have obliged; forgery could have been classed as a criminal offence if they had so chosen, and I might have finished the war in a civil prison. I was thankful that they had asked my partner and not me. It was always possible that I might have made a slip in putting pen to paper, and inadvertently given the show away. Our private papers and photos we put in used police envelopes, to be held until we were to leave their custody to be returned to our camp. (I still have mine, half a century on.)

We were then taken to the cells and thrust through separate opened doors in among the occupants gathered to see the new arrivals. They were for the most part French conscripted labourers whose crimes were principally work dodging. I had hardly had time to make myself a place to sleep in when the wail of the air-raid siren, which seemed to be mounted very near to us, shattered the comparative peace and abruptly put a stop to the lusty snoring of some of the sleepers who had not been disturbed by my entry to their quarters. We were, I was sure, in the top storey of the police headquarters, hardly a place of safety, but the French were in high glee at the thought of the RAF giving Germans a good going over! I could not share their delight. The only precaution taken on our behalf was a shouted instruction from one of the police telling us all to wake up, as if we could still be sleeping with the wail of sirens and excited chattering of the inmates of the cells. That duty done, the doors were slammed shut and we were left to our own devices. I had great difficulty in sharing the enthusiasm of the French, and was very relieved when we finally heard the continuous wail of the 'All clear'. The bombing had seemed to me too near to be healthy.

Our stay in that jail only lasted a couple of days, when a guard came to escort us back to Hohenfels. The first stage of our return journey was to Stalag V.A. Ludwigsburg where we were put in the *Flüchtlinge Abteilung* (escapers' section). Whether or not the rest of the inmates were escapees I had doubts, because the bulk of them were Dutch naval personnel, who, we were given to understand, had been called up to be put into prisoner of war camps for safe keeping. The Germans, anticipating the coming Second Front, were jittery and the incarceration of the Dutch made things a bit safer. All this arose, we were told, because the Dutch naval personnel had not been demobbed at the time of their country's defeat, but had been given indefinite leave. Double Dutch? It was to us at the time! Maybe it was our faulty interpretation of the explanation or, on the other hand, just another example of bureaucracy. What was the difference in reality between indefinite leave and demobilisation? In either case they had ceased to be a fighting force.

A few French and Polish were in this barrack, making up the number. We were a truly international throng. Our camp-made civilian clothes were exchanged for uniforms . . . French! These were well worn, tatty, and ill fitting. My trousers were cut in the cavalry style, reaching only to the calves, with their lower edges evidently intended to fit into the tops of laced-up riding boots. To make matters worse, along with them I inherited a colony of fleas. These seemed to delight in marching up and down my thigh, biting as they went. Something had to be done and quickly. Somehow or other I got hold of some chloride of lime and dosed them and my blankets with this powder. The results were drastic. Both my trousers and blankets were disintegrating by the following day and I had a weal on my thigh two to three inches wide and running the full length. My newly found Dutch friends organized an exchange of my offending garment and blanket and I found life more comfortable.

Our rations were principally potatoes, which, when mixed with apples that some of the more established inmates had procured, made quite a tasty meal. Bridge seemed to be the principal pastime of my little circle of friends, and I learnt the rudiments of this very absorbing game. More often than not our little sessions were of very international composition, comprising a Pole, a Dutchman, a Frenchman and myself; the bidding was in French! The expert among us was the Frenchman, who gave us a demonstration of an apparently impossible hand being played with such skill as to win with either a Grand Slam or a Small Slam, (if I remember the calls correctly, not having played that game since). He played it with all the cards face up on the table and went through the rigmarole of bidding evidently correctly and achieved the impossible. I wondered how he would have fared at my favourite game, poker.

During our short spell in that establishment we were joined by a New Zealander who related the circumstances of his capture; it was an almost unbelievable story, but I had no doubts about its truth. He had escaped from his camp and reached Lake Constance (Bodenzee), only to be picked up again. Giving his German guards the slip again, he had boarded the ferry. When it had reached about halfway across, he had been caught again within sight of freedom.

I suppose one of the highlights of our short stay in Ludwigsburg was the Dutch celebration of Queen Wilhelmina's birthday on 31 August. We might have been lacking in victuals, but not in enthusiasm in the impromptu concert that was put on for the occasion. We in our turn had to make a vocal contribution to the concert, and our rendering of the National Anthem was well received, not so much for the quality of our musical talent but for what our nation stood for in spite of our being on our own after Dunkirk. I am confident that all those in that POW camp that night realized that but for the British, Hitler would have enslaved all Europe and Russia by then. No wonder our European friends knew the words and joined in the singing so enthusiastically as if to verify the hope and confidence our little country had radiated throughout the dark days of Nazi dominance. A day or two later our guards arrived to escort us back to Stalag 383.

Chapter 27

Back in Camp

The journey was uneventful, yet in another way it could be described as a unique experience, in that not one of the four of us was speaking in his native tongue. George was doing his best with German to hold a conversation with a South African, while I struggled with my schoolboy French to converse with my Alsatian guard. To say the least, it was a peculiar set-up. The four of us sat chatting in a railway carriage, while the biggest holocaust in history was taking place, and half the world was embroiled in destruction. I could see, gazing through the train window when we passed through stations, the little groups of fresh cannon-fodder, conscripts waiting to be transported to take the place of the men lost on the various fronts Germany was fighting on. How many would survive? My thoughts went back to 1940, as we raced through Belgium to plug a hole in the line and passed Belgian conscripts waiting at bus stops on the same errand. Later, in 1941 and 1942, I had seen the same scenes in Czechoslovakia, and I knew well the same drama was taking place in England and indeed in over two-thirds of the world.

On our arrival back at Hohenfels we underwent the usual interrogation in the Commandant's office, where we were shown bullet-riddled dummies and told how foolish we were going over the wire. What had happened to the dummies could have easily happened to us! It did not take long for us both to realise that our captors had taken it for granted we had been involved with the attempt on the wire that had coincided with our exit via the main gate. We could cover our tracks for as long as the uniforms remained hidden in the wood near the station, and that meant the same format of escape could be used again.

After this interview, which was conducted in a quite amicable manner, we were led off to the bunker to serve our sentences of thirty days. The guards in our new billets were, to start with, very regimental. Indeed I had a row with one of them from the start. He insisted that I was only entitled to one blanket instead of the two I had been issued with. I argued with him and in the end threw one of them at him, all the time insisting that I was entitled to two. Later he came back and sheepishly handed me the offending blanket. After a day or two the guards were changed and their replacements were a decided improvement on the old ones. It did not take long before George and I had got round them; this was made easier because we were the only inmates in the place.

One way or another we were able to get extra food smuggled in along with fags, and life became quite passable. I even managed to get drawing materials – three large sheets of drawing paper – and set about sketching the story of my first venture into the big world beyond the wire. I aimed at about one hundred sketches in all. I pencilled out lines of each stage of the adventure and then inked them in with a mapping pen and Indian ink. The orderly officer who inspected the guard daily was very interested in my project and made a point of seeing how I was progressing every time he came. I mentioned my doubts about being able to keep this record when I rejoined my companions in the main camp, and he promised to see what he could do for me: a promise he fulfilled when that time came. To protect them from any scrutiny if the German personnel changed, he had each sheet stamped with the censor stamp (*geprüft*). Cheekily I made enquiries about sending them home, but naturally the powers that be would not entertain the idea – not that I thought they would. Between my cartoon strip and painting a view of the bunker in duplicate (one was for a guard), time passed pleasantly.

George did what cooking was necessary on a camp-made little stove that had been smuggled in to us. His culinary exploits were not without some near misses, which served to break the monotony. It was really funny when panic set in as the orderly officer was seen approaching and my 'chef' was vigorously fanning near the open window in an effort to get rid of smoke and the smell of cooking. It was not unusual to see the guards helping him; after all it was in their interest that we did not get caught.

Prisoner of war guard duty was very much preferable to the front; although I must point out that as the war progressed the fitness of our guards deteriorated as the Germans scraped the barrel. We heard some horrific stories from German soldiers who had served on the Russian Front: how their artillery had repelled Russian attacks, firing with open sights at the masses sent over with no turning back, seen to by their own commissars, who did not hesitate to mow down any who tried to retreat. It was common knowledge that troops in any way inferior were used by the 'Reds' to soak up the fire in most of their attacks. The terrific casualties they sustained were incredible to the Germans, as though they had a limitless source of more and more cannon-fodder. On the basis of many conversations that George and I had with Germans, we came to the conclusion that their main fear of Russia was its winter and vastness and the partisans who were for ever on their backs.

When we had done our time, we were returned to our former billets in the main camp. I did not return to my studies and the camp school, because I had been bitten again by the wander bug. I could not help thinking how easily we had walked out and left no trace of our method, leaving it open for another go. After a week or so, I was given marching orders, along with other former escapers. We had been quartered together in two huts opposite each other on the main camp road, which in theory made it easier to keep a watch on us. In hut 201, my new residence, were George Beeson; Fred Stuckey and Archie Mackee (two New Zealanders); Donald McDonald and Charley Elphick (Australians); Bill Tear and Bob Walker (Scottish); Ned Lynch (Irish); and Jim Dibble, Alex Shilton and Eric Hardman (English).

The security officer, Hauptman Katcherick, was a real gentleman and we almost felt sorry for him when we went about our business of plotting. In this scheming, we acted for the most part as individuals keeping our cards close to the chest whenever possible. This, I think was purely force of habit and did not reflect any distrust in our companions. Although we were under day and night surveillance, we got used to it and in no way did it hamper our activities.

The other security hut was opposite ours and contained hardened escapees, mostly from the Air Force. Although they were fellow conspirators pursuing the same goal as we were, we had very little contact with them.

Somehow, I don't know how, we succeeded in landing a plum camp job, that of unloading the bread wagons. Our unofficial pay for an hour or so's work, a bread loaf, was a princely reward, the normal ration being seven men to one loaf per day. Human nature being what it is, we were not satisfied with what we got legally and went to great lengths to relieve the Germans of as many loaves as circumstances permitted; normally at least two or three each, though there were times when we improved on this allocation. The bread store was nearer the main gate than the inner gate and we had to pass the guard on the inner gate to get back into camp. I often wondered what thoughts must have gone through the mind of whoever was on duty there as we trudged past with overcoats slung over our shoulder, bulging in the wrong places and sleeves stiffened with contents other than our arms. I cannot remember having any bother at that gate, although it was pretty obvious that we were bulkier on our return than when we went to work. We did have the odd panic when a German officer or warrant officer appeared on the scene when we were only half-way through the unloading.

On one such occasion we had to off-load our ill-gotten gains under the store shed, to be retrieved later with some difficulty. Another such panic came about when we were unloading the bread into a shed outside the wire and were searched on re-entering the camp. The lorry had been late and we were working at night, a filthy one at that, and as soon as we saw a search might be imminent, we pelted our swag over the wire where it was retrieved later on, mud stains and all. Unlike the lorry gang of Lamsdorf that I had worked with, these lads were not racketeers, and none of the loot was used for trading. No visitor to our hut went out hungry. I myself helped several mates I had known in the Yeomanry all through the time I was on that job, which lasted up to my next venture out of the wire.

My comrades in 201 were individualists, a truly mixed crowd of men with strong principles and one goal in mind, escape. This was invariably the principal topic of conversation, as were discussions on past experiences of breaking out. I resumed my free-lance penmanship for the camp official Escape Committee, doing odd jobs when required, and also my portrait sketching and painting, for which I never seemed short of sitters.

McDonald, one of the two Australians among our company, a plump, slow-speaking, slovenly man whose appearances belied his sharp brain and intellectual capabilities, had managed to get hold of some books on the Japanese language and a dictionary to go with them. Seeing the use a knowledge of that tongue could be, if and when the European side of the war was over, he set about studying it. The Japanese used the Chinese characters as a basis for their written words. Mac got me to try and help him sort out the system used to formulate their classification in the dictionary. No alphabet was used; each character was a collection of brush strokes. Along with his books was another on teaching oneself Chinese, which he passed on to me. My real study was learning the basic characters round which all Chinese was written; the pronunciation from phonetics was possibly harder than the written side, as far as I could see. Chinese had such a simple base of construction with virtually no rules of grammar. The spoken word was another matter with the intonation of the voice being the hardest to grasp from book learning. Japanese, from what Mac explained, was a very involved language, with so many different ways of addressing a person depending on his or her status. For me, remembering rules of grammar was far harder than remembering the character and how it was written, and my book on the subject was really simple to understand. I made a collection of cards with the character on one side and the meaning on the other, and gradually increased my knowledge by filling in odd moments by consulting them, as for instance when we were lined up for a lengthy roll call.

Chapter 28

Hooch

At about this time our hut organised a two up game on our bench-type table to raise funds. What profits were derived from our mini-casino went to the communal fund of our hut, as did most of the contents of our Red Cross parcels except for the chocolate, soap and fags. As not all of us were smokers, it was only fair that the use of these items was left to the individuals. I was only a casual user of the weed and valued fags for their trading power rather than as a sedative. I was even less interested in the 'hard stuff', when it was suggested some time later that we try our hands at distilling whisky. Beer was more in my line. I had only once ventured drinking spirits, when I had a shot at emptying a bottle of rum way back at Christmas of 1939, and finished up out for the count for nearly twenty hours. The real appeal this project had for me was curiosity and devilment rather than anything else, and I entered into the idea as keenly as the rest of the gang. We were not the originators of this idea and process. 'Hooch' could be bought on the market, and hardened drinkers went without food in their craving for it. Fortunately there were only one or two such men in the camp.

Out of our casino revenue we bought raisins and prunes, dried fruit that came in some of the Red Cross parcels, and added to them most of our own supplies of the same. In our own group we had one or two who, if they had not actually taken part in this illegal activity, nonetheless had sufficient knowledge of the process. An empty beer barrel was soon procured, and when sufficient fruit had been collected to fill the barrel to about a fifth of its depth, and enough wood assembled to fuel the process, along with the necessary amount of yeast to initiate the fermentation, our brewers decided to make a start.

In the course of obtaining our fuel we had made several night raids on an internal fence, removing alternate posts and stringing the wires together where the post had been. On our last raid, shots had been fired, fortunately without any casualties. Our own hierarchy in conjunction with our 'hosts' felt obliged to read the riot act to all the camp, pointing out the danger of this foolhardy behaviour. Bullets aimed at us were alleged to have finished up in some of the huts, luckily without hitting anyone. Needless to say, no more of that fence was removed; but neither were any of the culprits caught. The timber was well hidden under our hut. Another source of supply was a table removed from one of the offices in the outer compound by four of us acting as a fatigue party on 'official' instructions.

As well as this supply we had our legitimate firewood gathered by our representatives on the wood parties. These were organised foraging details that were marched out of the camp to the wooded areas nearby to collect fallen trees and dead wood to help eke out the meagre supply of coal we got for the hut stoves. Our representative on these foraging trips had a slight advantage over most of the party in the form of a saw. In its design it was rather peculiar, being in the form of a curve. I had a triangular file and set about making a saw out of the only piece of steel I could come by, a barrel hoop. It was not a design I would recommend, but provided the user synchronised his arm action with the curve of the hoop and was not too impatient, it achieved something like the desired result. While the guards were supervising the gathering of dead wood, they were inclined, with our help, to pay more attention to the taste of a bit of English chocolate and the luxury of a good cigarette, than to the crazy antics of a couple of men with a bent saw.

The start to the brewing involved the boiling of many jugfuls of water. We used the standard aluminium one holding about 1½ gallons with which every hut was equipped. This went on until the fruit in the barrel was covered. Yeast was then floated on toast on the surface of the brew. A cover was put over the barrel and a watch kept on the contents as it took about ten days before the fermentation gave signs of diminishing, showing that it was time to start distillation.

In the meanwhile, our technical team had been busy rigging up the still. The container was one of the standard camp jugs which had been fitted with a lid. The condenser and other attachments we borrowed from the 'professionals'. The condenser had been made from copper piping, (of the same bore as that used on motorcycles), and was fitted into a water jacket made from three soldered Canadian dried-milk tins. A small tin bath was placed underneath to catch the water that was continuously being poured over this crude form of condenser. The process started with the jug on the stove, the contents of which had to be kept at a steady temperature and depth. This was one man's job, with another man watching the delivery end and endeavouring to maintain a steady drip out of the condenser. Anything more than drops would be condensed water. Once this process had started it could not be stopped on any account, and went on round the clock.

We knew the security patrol would pay us a visit during the night, and sure enough they did, in the early hours. In reply to their questioning, we assured them that we were making wine, and that we would show the Hauptman, if necessary, the apparatus in the morning. Fortunately we were never put to the test, and immediately the process was finished, the apparatus was taken back to the makers. The product was colourless, and to give it the appropriate whisky colour, burnt sugar was added. Each of us got a bottle and half a mug. Its potency was soon evident when several of our company burst into song after sampling the oddment in their mugs! The rendering Archie Mackee and Ned Lynch gave of 'Beautiful Dreamer' is still ringing in my ears fifty years on. It had been the intention of most of our number to keep the bulk of the product of our labours for Christmas, which was only a week or so off; but the thrifty subsidised the impatient when Christmas came. How we managed it I do not know, but for our celebration of the New Year, which our two Scots regarded as more important, a fair-sized barrel of beer had come into our possession.

In anticipation of the Second Front I made a Union flag, which we put up on the gable end of the roof of our hut on the stroke of midnight with a bit of a noisy ceremony. Our guards ignored our merry-making, and our flag flew for twenty-four hours before we took it down without incurring any trouble from our 'hosts'. I had made it from some linen-like material from a New Zealand personal parcel, starting off with ink dyes which ran. To cover this blotting of the ink it was necessary to get some more of the material and sew strips with folded edges on both sides of the flag, taking particular attention with the positioning of the broad and narrow widths. It was a very tricky job, and with the hems on both sides I was sewing through five thicknesses. After it had served its purpose on New Year's Eve it was cut up and all in 201 got a piece.

Chapter 29

Itchy Feet Again

After this brief respite from our main preoccupation, the itchy feet became active again and our numbers depleted at intervals. First Eric Hardman disappeared and soon after my erstwhile companion in field grey, George Beeson. George made his way out by the simple expedient of exchanging places with one of the French detainees who formed fatigue parties from their camp down the road to do some of the mundane jobs in our camp. That exchange was a comparatively easy job. The two would meet in the latrine and exchange tunics, coats and headgear, and George would join the working party of French while his exchange would join us in 201. Once outside our camp, George would take advantage of the free and easy way the French were kept. In our discussions, I had pointed out my reservations on this scheme: slackness in a working party was not necessarily reflected in the outside world. Travelling in the role of a Frenchman would be particularly tricky, because George to the best of my knowledge, knew no French. He maintained, however, that the French themselves had little desire to return to France, because all the north of their country was under the jackboot, and while the south was supposedly under French control, the puppet Vichy government was for the most part in the hands of pro-German French. As far as I could weigh up the chances, everything depended on an early contact with the partisans.

George was not the only one in our camp to use this exchange. By the end of the year we had five French living among us. They presented no difficulty for us as long as their exchanges remained free; but once any one was caught and brought back to camp, we had a spare Frenchman to hide whenever there was a roll call and check up. That was not the end of the matter; there was the little detail of food, particularly as the year wore on and our rations shrank and we became more and more dependent on the Red Cross parcels.

Early in the year a novel escape plan was hatched in our hut. We had observed that a small truck came to the cookhouse regularly as clockwork every Saturday evening. The plan was to steal it, and with two of us aboard in German gear and the rest under a tarpaulin in the back, make off with it. Checks on the timing were made and it was seen that the gate guard was very casual, rarely stopping it as it left the camp. A start was made on collecting petrol; indeed, as time went on our hut became a veritable fire risk with bottles of the stuff arranged round the room behind the beds. Two Australian tunics were arranged and progress was made on the German outfits. With all these preparations being attended to, we reached the point of naming the crew and hit a real problem then. I was to be crew commander, simply because of my limited knowledge of the language. My partner was most likely to be Charley Elphick, one of the Australians, because of his driving experience. The rest were to hide under tarpaulins in the back, as it was an open truck. From time to time we had heard someone in the cookhouse playing a piano accordion, music that we might need as a diversion when starting the truck up. The most probable way of getting it going with the minimum of noise was to push it well clear of the cookhouse. These were problems to be sorted out when we had settled the preliminaries, the main one of which was the crew. The truck would not hold all of us, but the man we had doubts about was as keen as the rest. The problem was our proposed handling of the real driver and his mate if they tumbled to our little scheme and attempted to stop us. We wanted to avoid physical violence if possible, preferably by getting a good start before they realised their motor had gone. If necessary we would have to kidnap them and take them with us bound and gagged to be dumped near civilization. However, the member whose possible actions frightened us could not be dropped out of the scheme without our being frank with him, which would mean telling him that he was punch drunk. The more we toyed with different schemes to dissuade him, the more determined he became, and in the end we dropped the idea.

Having two German uniforms going begging was bound to put ideas into my head, and I connived with the intended wearer of the other one, Charley Elphick, the tall Australian who was as keen as myself. In the middle of our planning, I was taken off to the camp hospital with a bad dose of piles – haemorrhoids – and operated on almost immediately.

I well remember the embarrassing operation, with my legs wide open in some sort of a metal frame, I had a local anaesthetic and consequently heard all that went on, the snipping of scissors and the chatter of the doctor and his assistant. That was not all though. In the room next to mine one of the doctors, a budding musician, was learning to play the violin, and his choice of piece was 'God save the King'. The hospital was clean and warm with quite good beds, unlike the French-run one in 1940, and I could have really enjoyed a short spell there; but it was not to be. I was discharged the following day to face the rigours of winter back in my old barrack. There was worse to come after a day or so, when I had to put this offending part of my anatomy to the test. A prison camp is not the ideal place to convalesce, nor are its latrines, with their rows of seats along the outer walls and centre back-to-back accommodation, the last word in privacy. They had one very important thing in their favour, however: they were clean.

A minor detail of a damaged rectum was not going to deter me from our projected excursion, and so our preparations started again from where we left off. McCallam and his organisation had found me the run of numbers on the passes, and also discovered a major change in them: there was now a photo in true passport style of the bearer in the square provided, instead of the rubber-stamped impression on the original ones. This presented no bother. We were not short of photographers or photographic materials in the camp. Charley and I reported to a safe hut and, complete with medal-bedecked *Wehrmacht* uniforms, were photographed in the true passport manner. My one regret was that I never got a print of either photo and to make it more disappointing, I had promoted myself to *Feldwebel* (sergeant) since the last time I had worn field grey or should I say, field green?

Bit by bit we were getting nearer to taking-off time. The papers had to be left to the last before completing the dating and numbering; any slip in departure time would have made them useless. The day arrived and the date was significant, 17 March, St Patrick's

Day. It had a special meaning to me, and my thoughts went back to 1940, when we were waiting in Northern France for the real war to start. I was in an Irish regiment, the 5th Royal Inniskilling Dragoon Guards, and we wore the shamrock. The following day I started off for home leave, feeling proud to have been accepted as an equal in such a famous regiment. Before this I and my fellow NCOs from the East Riding Yeomanry had been 'weekend soldiers' attached, but now we were officially posted. Like them, I had started by wearing the Tank Corps badge; then at the outbreak of war we were to become the East Riding Yeomanry, and now I was a Dragoon (horseless). These thoughts ran through my head as Charley and I were being dressed in the safe hut I had used for the same purpose with George Beeson seven months before. We made our way to the guard on the first gate, showed him our passes, and were let through with no bother. Once again I found myself on the nine o'clock walk, when, as before, every step was taking me and Charley to the real test of our nerves, our rig-out, our papers, mannerisms and coolness. Without saying a word, I took off one of my black leather gloves and reaching into my left breast pocket for my pass, showed it to the guard. He acknowledged it and saluting, gave it me back, and turned his attention to my Australian friend as I continued on through the gate. Immediately there was a bit of a rumpus. Spinning round to see what the trouble was, I shouted in a voice as official as I could make it, 'Was ist los?' ('What's up?').

It was no use trying to bluff. Whether it was Charley's lack of German or not, this guard was on the ball. With his rifle levelled at us in his right hand and the telephone in his left, he was shouting down it loud enough not to have need of it. His reinforcements were soon on the scene, headed by a real *Feldwebel* brandishing his automatic and shouting to me, as the senior non-commissioned officer of the 'two', that he was an old enemy of England. Here he pointed to his last war ribbons. We were marched to the guard room, where the Germans seemed to be most concerned with our passes and in particular our photos. It seemed to me they could not decide whether they were genuine passes stolen from the camp office, and the photos of actual Germans, with ourselves picked because we looked very much like them; or whether, on the other hand, they were good forgeries. We for our part were too annoyed at being caught so early to be apprehensive about our fate. The outcome was that we were stripped of the offending outfits and searched, and then, still in our civilian suits, that we had on under our disguise, we were marched to the bunker. Our impression of the whole affair was that the Germans treated it as a normal escape attempt meriting the usual thirty days in the cooler.

It was only some time after, when we thought back on it, that we realised our attempt could have merited a term in a *Straflager*, or even worse, a firing squad. I will not say we were not scared for a while, but somehow their antics with the passes and the absence of physical violence allayed our fears. Maybe they were heartily sick of the war and had some sympathy for us prisoners.

During our time in the bunker we were paid a visit by the guard who had tumbled to Charley. He told us he had been given fourteen days' leave for his alertness and the unfortunate guard who had let us through the first gate had been rewarded with fourteen days in prison.

Our bunker warders started off by being 'regimental', but we soon converted them and, being the only guests, soon had the routine organised so that our stay in that establishment was made as comfortable as possible for all. Things were, of course, made easier with the aid of our cohabitants of 201. As on my last stretch in this building, which I shared with George Beeson, I had access to drawing materials, which enabled me to set about making a pictorial story of the trip to Stuttgart in 1943. Once again my efforts were of interest to the orderly officer as he did his rounds, and, as I had managed last time, I was fortunate when I came out to have them stamped with the censor clearance mark. Our release came on 12 April, we rejoined our mates in 201, and I resumed my freelance work for the Escape Committee whenever my services were required for passports or papers.

The war was hotting up with the prospect of the Second Front being launched at any time, and the Germans was getting edgy. Proof of this was to be seen in the posters put up in the camp warning of the new threat escapers faced. They described attempted escape as 'a damned dangerous sport', and assuring all that any evaders caught in certain areas of security, of which Hohenfels was one, would be summarily shot on capture. This reaction had been brought about by the Allies' use of commandos and saboteurs. I would not suggest that this deterred any of the regulars giving it a go, but rather, as the war in Europe crept nearer our way and the bombing reached Nürnburg only thirty miles away, it was common sense to be a bit more patient and not go headlong into it. Our food moreover was drastically cut down, in part because of shortages created by the shrinking Nazi perimeter, and also because of the great losses in rolling stock created by the bombing of marshalling yards and the railway in general. The morale in the camp had never been higher, while physique deteriorated through lack of food.

Christmas 1944 was very bleak with the worsening food and parcel situation, but the news was a real shot in the arm to our spirits. Our information came from the wireless in the main, although we did get first-hand accounts of happenings at home and on the Second Front from new prisoners joining our ranks. All special announcements over the British wireless were taken down by our shorthand writers, then copies were printed on a make-shift Roneo and circulated to each company in the camp. A reader would then call on all the huts he had allocated to his company and read out the most important items of news word for word, particularly Churchill's speeches.

Chapter 30

Evacuating 383

As time went on and we were into April, food conditions worsened and the effects of semi-starvation showed on the faces of many of the less hardy ones among us. Not only did they become gaunt but their skin had a greyish tinge. Starvation does not kill its victims quickly but makes them more susceptible to ailments that normally they would have shrugged off. Rumours were rife, especially those concerning delivery of life–preserving Red Cross parcels. We were told strenuous efforts were being made to get these through from Switzerland. They did eventually reach us by road in a fleet of white-painted lorries which we christened 'The White Angels'. Although they were not in sufficient numbers to be issued as intended, one parcel a week per man, we still appreciated getting one to two men. By now the bread ration was ten men to a loaf instead of the normal seven.

Other rumours that had been going the rounds were of a more disturbing nature, such as the possibility of hard cores of Nazis using this part of the *Vaterland* to retreat to because of its rocky terrain; it might even come to their using us as hostages. With this in mind a movement got going to defend ourselves if the necessity arose. In our midst were men of all branches of the army, and schemes were prepared to take over the camp armed with anything we could collect if the Germans decided to do anything drastic. We realised we were in the middle of a military training area, with the potential danger that implied, but judged that any sort of action was better than being sitting targets for German reprisals. This situation never materialised fortunately, but with Patton getting nearer every day and the Germans being driven back, it was obvious that our liberation must come in a few days. Rumour had it that in view of the approach of the fast-moving American 5th Army, we were to be shifted. This was one rumour that proved to be right.

Moving quickly, the Germans assembled the first party of about 1,500 by the single expedient of employing troops from the training area. A second batch was to go the following day, and the remainder the day after. Getting the first batch together had not presented too much difficulty because of the element of surprise. The second batch was not quite so easy, but apparently the assistance of our own disciplinary leaders had been sought and promised. In the ensuing turmoil men were running all over the place to keep out of the line-up, but, with the aid of some of our own leaders and police, enough were assembled to follow in the steps of the first lot. The following day was to see the camp emptied except for the sick in the hospital, and of course the malingerers; as the day wore on another group of stay-behinds appeared in dribs and drabs. These were the occupants of the two security huts, who had scattered round the camp and hid in a variety of places. I myself had spent one day in the false roof of the cookhouse until our military police tried to force a group of us to join the main throng, when we had had to scatter. In the process one of the cooks had given me a military police armband which enabled me to reach the hut under the floor of which most of my cronies were hiding. I had virtually been chased by an MP for my armband when he realised I was an imposter. I obliged by taking it off and throwing it at him.

The hut we were under was of the type standard throughout the camp. It was built in sections on a wooden floor which stood on concrete blocks about fifteen inches off the ground. Weeds and undergrowth masked the area underneath the floor on the outside, and inside the hut, bunks, a table and two platform seats had been tipped over to make entry impossible. Some home-made box furniture completed the general chaos. Once or twice a guard poked his head round the door, and seeing the wreckage, thought twice about entering, muttered aloud some obscenity and left, little knowing how near he was to us, and maybe eternity. Under the floorboards supporting the wreckage, I was scared someone would sneeze; if any of the Germans had ventured in, pressure on the floor would have surely disturbed the dust. On each of these nerve-racking visits the only noise we made was the throb of our heart beats or so it seemed, such was the tension. We were not to be thwarted in our efforts to get free at this late stage, and I am sure any attempt by the guards to take us would have resulted in bloodshed. My thoughts went back to the episode in the working compound at Lamsdorf, when one of our party was threatened as he walked to the latrine by a guard rattling his rifle bolt.

A partial solution to our food supply passed by outside the wire in the shape of a Ukrainian shepherd with his herd. Within minutes the wire was breached, and five minutes later we had a skinned carcase hidden behind a coat on the back of the hut door. Minutes later a German poked his head into the hut and made futile enquiries about some sheep that had been stolen, a matter about which we knew nothing, of course! After sharing in a brew of tea and being consoled by an English fag, he departed.

That night three of us set off with sacks of boots, shoes and clothing, shirts and pullovers for the most part that we were taking to the village to trade for food. Most of this gear had been left in huts vacated in the last three days. We made our way across the sports field which had only a single wire fence that was easily dealt with, and set off on our trading mission to the little village which gave its name to the camp. The night was clear as day with the bright moonlight as we tramped with our sacks full of merchandise. My thoughts went back to nearly two years before when Beeson and myself had walked out of the main gate on the other side of the camp. The route this night was more or less directly opposite the one we had taken to get to the station at Parsberg, and as far as we were concerned, was in territory completely unknown to us. My reflections were suddenly disturbed by the regular sound of marching men, who seemed to be getting nearer and nearer. The best cover we could find was in the shadow of a massive outcrop of rock. We hardly dared breathe as we remained motionless listening to the rhythmic sound getting nearer and nearer; then we wondered if we were mistaken, for the sound seemed to have changed direction and was getting fainter and fainter, until we could only hear the noises we were producing as we walked stealthily on.

It was not long before we were stepping out, noise or no noise. It was by now midnight and most of the village was in darkness.

As could only be expected most of the population would be in bed. We tried knocking on the doors of some of the houses where chinks of light could be seen, signifying that somebody was still up. When any of the doors was opened, it was easy to see that our trading mission was too late to do any good. For one thing those that answered our knock were too scared to do any business, obviously being too frightened of us, or thinking that our efforts were some trick of the *Gestalt* or imagination. Disappointed with our failure, we were in a bit of a quandary over our next move when we came across a farmyard barn with a ladder leading up to a sort of hayloft. It was a likely place to bed down. We climbed the ladder and stretched out in the straw. No sooner had we done this when a German with a hurricane lamp entered the building and climbed the ladder until he was within reaching distance of the hay. He grabbed as much as he could carry under one arm, and muttering to himself, descended the ladder and made off into the blackness of the building. By the sound of it, he must have had a horse and was giving it supper. We maintained silence for a while and then when we thought it safe to whisper, we agreed to have a sleep and then set off early back to the camp.

We were up early and vacated the place without seeing anybody. On the way back we encountered a bullock wagon driven by a Frenchman and hitched a lift on it. This form of transport must be the slowest in the world, but we were in no hurry, we had to wait for the Americans to reach the camp. Later in the day we explored the main camp's office belonging to the commandant, where I found a very good box camera and about fifty films. I made a cardboard box to hold it in always at the ready on my chest, and had one or two films in my pockets. The following day we made another excursion as hopefuls, this time in daylight and full view. On our way we passed a German military policeman at a crossroads who appeared to be waiting to welcome the Yanks. He seemed to be completely uninterested in our presence there.

Further on we were about to pass a farmhouse that stood at the roadside with the front door open, and thinking that I might get some information about the situation in that area, I called out. Getting no reply I went in and through an open doorway on the right saw a couple of Germans sitting at an empty table, looking absolutely dejected. For want of something better to say, I asked them for a light. They replied that they did not have one, and told me to go into the room opposite. At first this appeared to be empty, until I turned to look to my left. On a bench seat up to the wall was an old lady sitting bolt upright. I could only presume it was her wake, because I did not have to look twice to see that she was dead, and had been for a day or two. I beat a hasty retreat to my waiting company outside and lit my fag myself; I needed it.

It was obvious to us that Patton's army was meeting resistance in that part of Bavaria. Those few Germans we had seen were obviously waiting to give themselves up. Further on we came across several wooden buildings and found out that they were used to house refugees from Hamburg and other heavily bombed cities. After talking to one of these unfortunates, we were told that her hut had been knocked about by other escaped prisoners, most of the damage being doors wrenched off their jambs. I think our actions in rehanging them and finding a bit of chocolate for her children did a lot to compensate for the petty spite our compatriots had shown. Finding one of these dwellings empty, we transfered our gear and set up camp there, where we were joined by other POWs. Food was not easily come by, but we managed, and found we had an excellent cook who excelled himself in his gastronomic concoctions.

On one of our foraging or trading trips we met up with a Hungarian corporal, who exchanged some of the stores his unit, a service one, was transporting for pyjamas and a suitcase for his lady friend. His unit was using horse-drawn vehicles, a form of transport the Germans had used throughout the war, in spite of all the modernisation of the rest of their war-making equipment. Our Hungarian business acquaintance told us he was expecting to be on the move any time; he had no idea where to, but he naturally hoped it would be Hungary.

Chapter 31

Patton's Army

The following day, Sunday, 22 April 1945, was to be the long-awaited day of liberation, with the arrival of an American jeep at 4.02 p.m., bearing campaign scars and a bullet-holed wind-screen. This event must have just about emptied the camp hospital, judging by the number of 'invalids' who turned out. There was no doubt in our minds that the ranks of patients had been swelled when the camp was being evacuated. We wondered how many genuine sick had been prevented from receiving proper treatment or worse still, been forced to join the marchers, because of those able-bodied individuals seeking this less hazardous form of evasion.

While this local excitement was going on, the main thrust of Patton's army continued and units were going through Hohenfels where we had established ourselves. Gathering what gear we could carry back, we went to our new depot, having decided to get clear of the official repatriation organisation and make our own way back, hopefully in American empty transport. By now they were coming through the village at regular intervals, preceded by their tanks and tank destroyers. Their billeting officers were meanwhile seeking out spare accommodation for their local troops. We even saw a town crier at work announcing the instructions of the occupying force to the local inhabitants. We spent a couple of nights in our local quarters. When empty transport started to come through, we waited our opportunity to make use of it, gathered by a camp fire we had lit at the roadside.

It was not long before help came in the shape of an articulated refrigerated lorry. By this time I had been joined by other POWs and had lost touch with most of my previous companions. After chatting with the driver and his mate who told me they were returning to Frankfort empty and we were welcome to have a lift, we were installed in the spacious back of the vehicle and on the first leg of the journey home. Travelling with the rear doors swung back, we were in high spirits as we watched the landscape changing behind us. After an hour or so we stopped, and our friends from the United States produced food in the form of packages labelled 'one man seven days/seven men one day'. The contents included food and drink, cigarettes, sweets and even toilet paper. Things had certainly changed during our incarceration.

Our next stop was a little German town, name unknown, (we were too excited to bother to find out!). Here we were billeted in a house whose inhabitants were an old couple scared out of their wits as a coloured American sergeant demanded accommodation for us. As a precautionary measure, which must have added to their fear, we were lent a couple of Tommy guns. After assuring our reluctant hosts that we meant no harm to them, we settled down where we were, taking care not to make any mess.

In the morning, before continuing our journey, we left them all we had in the way of food, including one or two packets of tea. Continuing on our way we reached Frankfort (on the Main) at about twelve noon, and freshened up in a big public underground toilet near the main buildings the Americans had taken over. In my eagerness to get moving, I walked into a barbed wire fence that surrounded this subterranean facility and gashed the bridge of my nose. With one hand trying to stem the flow of blood with a handkerchief, I sat down in the large dining hall to sample the delights of a GI's lunch. What I ate, or how I managed, I cannot remember, but I do recollect the attention I and my pals drew from that assembly of diners. The building we were in was some sort of shopping emporium, and after the meal we were shown our billets for the night on a higher floor equipped with rows of camp beds, where we were allocated ours. Leaving our gear behind, more or less as markers, we were escorted to a nearby park where we watched a game of baseball until it was time to return for our evening meal.

Afterwards we joined little groups of the GIs and were bombarded with questions about our experiences as prisoners of war. We found our new friends were predominantly Texans and their unit a service supply column, after the style of our own Royal Army Service Corps. In due course, I tore myself away from them and was soon in bed reflecting on the last few hectic days and the prospect of being home soon in my own bed!

I was soon asleep, but not for long. I woke suddenly to find I was the centre of attraction and surrounded by a small crowd of soldiers round my bed. The ones nearest me were trying to assure me that I was among friends and alright. It appeared that I had had a nightmare and had been shouting in my sleep something about being in the hands of the Gestapo. I had no recollection of dreaming. After a while I managed to convince the gathering that I was fine, they dispersed and I resumed my sleep.

The following morning I was sure I was the object of attention by some of those whom I had alarmed the previous night. We washed and shaved in a large washroom and our friends from 'Over There' played up because there was no hot water. I could not help thinking that before they got home again, they would be very lucky if that was all they had to complain about.

Having smartened ourselves up, we went down to have our breakfast. This was more like a banquet; pancakes and syrup followed by eggs, bacon and fried bread and so on. They certainly were well fed, but I could not get the one thing I most wanted, a cup of tea. However, their coffee was the real thing and not the ersatz German stuff.

Chapter 32

Home via Paris

After breakfast we had not long to wait before we were saying our good byes and on the next leg of our journey to blighty. This time our conveyance was a fifteen hundred-weight open truck and our destination Paris, a ride of something like four hundred miles. I positioned myself at the back near the tail-board and as usual was looking for opportunities to use my camera. The scene from the back of that truck was one of almost continuous devastation of war: shattered buildings, broken-down or blown-up vehicles and now and then bridges with temporary repairs to allow the passage of road vehicles over them, albeit at a crawl. Busy road junctions had, for the most part, a traffic controller, either civil or military police. After three or four hours' travel, we halted for the first stop and coffee.

The place was Rheims, and we were about half way to our destination, Paris. I must have been impatient, because I had left my greatcoat on a low wall near the truck when we stopped, and after the short break at the café, I clean forgot it until we were well clear of the place. I was annoyed with myself, not so much for the loss of the coat, but for the regimental badges it carried. However worse things happen in war and I was privileged to be a survivor and on my way home.

The rest of the journey was uneventful. Roundabout tea-time we entered the outskirts of the French capital. It was a hive of activity, with people and soldiers milling about everywhere, not to mention the military vehicles that jammed the roads. It was obvious that our driver and his mate had been to Paris before, and more than once, judging by the way we picked a route through it all to finish up outside a small hotel where they fixed us up for the night and a meal. Leaving us to our own devices for the evening, they promised to call round in the morning to arrange a flight to England on one of their empty transport planes. They were as good as their word and after a sound night's sleep and a French breakfast, we were taken to Le Bourget airport, full of expectations of being in England before the morning was out. To our great disappointment, however, we were told low clouds had prevented our plane taking off, and we would have to wait for an improvement in the weather.

In our wanderings round the airport buildings we were noticed by an RAF officer who, when he found out our true identity, organised us to be taken over by our own people. That in turn made for a longer delay, but rules are rules and we had to wait for the red-tape wheels to revolve. We thanked our GI friends and that was the last we saw of them.

A British ladies organisation took us over and did their best to keep us entertained, showing us the more sedate sights of the French metropolis. We visited Napoleon's tomb to which the coffin containing his son's remains had been moved from its resting place befitting his rank of King of Rome on the orders of Hitler, we were told. Leaving Les Invalides, we went next to the Arc de Triomphe at the end of the famous Champs Elysées. This massive triumphal arch houses the French unknown warrior's remains and has a perpetual flame. Other sights included the Trocadero Gardens and Eiffel's famous tower. Had we not been in such a hurry to get home, we should have enjoyed this sightseeing much more. To round this trip off, we were taken to a 'Palm Court' – style restaurant for afternoon tea and cakes complete with the appropriate-style orchestra. The ladies really gave us the red carpet treatment.

The evening and night found us in small groups roaming round the city with its varied places of entertainments lit up as though there was no war on. Uniforms predominated everywhere, particularly the American ones. For our part, sightseeing was its own entertainment as we wandered round, and in any case we had no money. For my part I was only too impatient to get home again to have been interested in the night life for which Paris is renowned.

The following morning we were once again taken to Le Bourget airport and boarded a Dakota for the next lap of our return home.

We had a good flight without incident and although most of us had never flown before, we had no need for recourse to the paper bags we were issued with. The first sight of that strip of water that had stopped the Germans in 1940 was for me a very emotional moment; I am sure I was not the only one.

We landed at an airport in Buckinghamshire and the army took over then. We were individually interrogated and then given ration cards, some money and travel warrants, after a medical check-up and a good dinner. Transport was provided to the station. Some time later I arrived at King's Cross where I boarded a train for Hull after sending a telegram home, with the words, 'Home to-night. Vies'.